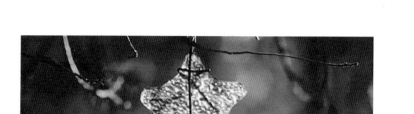

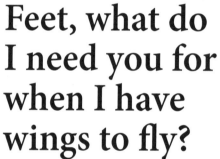

Feet, what do
I need you for
when I have
wings to fly?

—Frida Kahlo

Printed and bound in the United States.
Paperback: ISBN- 978-1530071555

Editors
Sara Hess
Richard Rogers
Carol Teelin
Jamie Ramirez

Cover and Book Design
Deb DeAugistine

Cover and Author Photos
Jeffrey Foote Photography

Jessica is from Ithaca, New York, the heart of Leyla's Village. Leyla is traveling freely in the Great Beyond and lives in our hearts. She calls the whole universe home.

Leyla's Dedication

What is life, if not love?
What is life, if not the moments
that take your breath away?
What is life, if not the shimmering
full love that leaves one breathless.
Life is simply beauty and beauty is simply bliss,
a pure and endless stream.

This past year has taught me who I am, and brought me to those who helped me find myself. This book is dedicated to two people that I could never live without. The people I go home to and wake up to every morning; to my darling sister Opal Juliana and my incredible mother, Julia Dietrich.

Opal, watching you grow is the most incredible thing that I will ever experience. I remember holding you in my arms, your tiny hand grabbing my finger; how delicate you were. You are my sassy little love. There is never a dull moment, and I never cease to laugh when I am with you. It is you I will always watch over, no matter where I am. Thank you for filling my life with laughter. My sister you will always be.

To my dearest Momma, you are my heart. Thank you for shining your light on the darkest of days, holding my hand in the scariest of moments, and being your incredible self. Thank you for being my rock and pulling me up when I think the world is crashing down. This ride of life would not be the same without the two of you. You make my world lovely and bright. You are my heart.

Sending Love,

Leyla

Foreward

This book is a love story grounded in truth and in this earth. It is about the life and death of my young sweet friend, Leyla. It is not a work of fiction; rather it is a collection of existential musings that have delighted us with delicate life lessons. We composed this collection from a raw and humble place, over a span of two years, from her diagnosis to her final breath. What lies within are our unfiltered emotions and experiences and how we sought happiness, hope and healing of heart.

This was co-authored in a most organic way. Leyla had entrusted me fully to bring about the truth she wished to share. She gave me the gift of sharing her story with the world, and in doing so had awakened a sleeping giant within me, a giant that was hungry for words, long stories, meaningless things, and unhurried journeys. We wrote, however, like people on borrowed time, because we were. As a result of these matters of time, many of our initial thoughts had not fully manifested themselves into story-hood. So, I have returned to these writings, and worked to fill in spaces that would otherwise leave readers confused and disconnected.

We created this work for you, and because it is our deepest and most profound form of truth, we wish to convey the honesty in which that truth grew. Leyla would often text or call me saying "I love you Jessi. Can you come over tomorrow so we can write?" In this manner, I am a simple harvester of words, making only the slightest adjustments to what she has written to ensure that the story of her life and the meaning she wished to convey is fully alive within. Leyla's voice is within every molecule of every thought, intention and action inside of these pages; when her actual words are used they will be differentiated from my narrative using yellow- or blue-colored pages.

In many ways, I was Leyla's Sherpa mother, guiding her safely through a temporal and universal abyss to find the meaning of her existence perfectly distilled in inky blackened words. I was a baby fledging warrior, clearing dusty cobwebs and meaningless conversations she wished to discard, gathering and grounding her safely as she walked between words and worlds.

Leyla came quickly to recognize the purpose of her life in this world for the divine nature of the universe had awakened inside of her, calling her softly to return home. I am deeply blessed and humbled by the gift of narrating this story, and offer a simple dedication.

Leyla, daughter of my heart and Michael, my gentle bear-child, loving you both has been the loveliest of heartaches. You have broken my heart wide open to the beauty in the world, and all of the wisdom it has to offer. You inhabit every breath I breathe, always know that I hold your heart snuggled close to mine. You have been the greatest teachers of my life, and I am so lucky to have plucked you from the universal cauldron of perfect human creature children. I love you both the biggest of all.

This dedication would not be complete without acknowledging the rest of my tribe and Leyla's Village. You are earth, gravity and all of the elements, and I love each and every one of you to distraction.

Big love,

Jessica

Writing Nest

The Hive

The Hive is often how we describe the inner most workings of the village. While we could not possibly reflect all our loved ones in this ever-changing and shifting manifestation of love, we have captured a few of our shiniest treasures that comprise the story within these pages.

ALI Rich's sister and Katie's sister-in law, so cute we often want to scoop her up and carry her in our pockets where we can hear her beautiful laughter all day long. She is our resident esthetician, making us shine bright and lovely, all the while twisting our hair in the most elaborate braids.

AMY C Leyla's best friend, 1/3 of Leyla's whole, completely comfortable at the bottom of a cuddle puddle with her Leyla and her Meli. Our artist- she tattoos her young life journey deeply under her skin in beautiful blackened lines. Our very own ink-apprentice-in-the-making and the designer of many of our L4 tattoos.

AMY STONE aka My Amy - Julia's best friend, Jessica's sister, healer extraordinaire. Once introduced Papa's motorcycle to an apple tree. In adolescence, lived in an apartment in College Town with Julia and Katie where they caused absolutely no trouble at all. Calls all of us "Bitches" before 6:00 a.m. on nursing exam days, and no one quite seems to mind. In fact, Melynda supports her vulgarity by saying, as long as she does well, "she can slap my ass and call me Sally." So, name calling also = LOVE in village speak.

AUGIE/AUGUST Leyla's cousin, Katie's youngest child, oldest of the tinies, future head of theirmotorcycle club. Leyla loved to photograph Augie, and captured his delicious, naked, chubby, laughing self in so many shots. My favorite Augie-ism of all time: "Why did the angels take she (Leyla)?"

AYSIA Jamon's second-born who basked in the love of a big sister for such a short time. Our girl with mad writing skills, she can find her way through poetry like no other, but not through a pile of dishes. Oh no, dishes are the lost art of chore.... though she may write a Haiku about it.

BLIND SPOTS Band composed of our beautiful Miss Maddy and our beloved Resident Muscians. Creators/collaborators of our all-time favorite theme songs: Make you Happy & Leyla's Song.

CHUCKIE Family friend of all persons Dietrich since forever. Flower whisperer, and purveyor of wishes, swimming pools and baby elephants.

DR. KORONES Leyla's Oncologist. Gentle man and wizard with the power of gifting precious time. Every time Leyla spoke his name, "I love, love, LOVE him!" followed in her sweet, happy voice.

EMMA Amy's older daughter, rivals Opal only when it comes to fashion and vanity. Stepping is her main love, and whenever she is upright she is engaged in some form of beautiful movement. It makes watching her brush her teeth very entertaining.

ENRIQUE Melynda's husband, Mr. Easygoing, always happy to go along for the ride, or take Julia's trash out at 10:00 pm on the eve of garbage day.

ESLETS Julia and Jamon's twins, refers to Esmae and Violet paired, the name dreamed into existence by Aysia.

ESMAE Julia's daughter, the younger of the twins - our little soul salve, her smile the light of the village. Her bright, big almond eyes, watch every single thing in the gloriously wide world. Our dark-skinned beauty, she gave us reason to believe that even in darkness, love blooms in beautiful abundance.

GUN POETS Our peaceful warrior rappers Dan (Rising Sun) and Josh (JayHigh) and our beloved Resident Musicians. Creators/ collaborators of our all-time favorite theme songs: Make you Happy & Leyla's Song.

JARED Leyla's first and only love. My Amy told Leyla she should fall in love and learn to drive before leaving this world. Who could have known that love as its most profound depths would manifest itself in her lifetime? It was as if one moment there was Jared and there was Leyla, individual teenagers curious about the nature of being alive. And then there was Jared and Leyla , who seemingly fell in love in a singular moment in between the bars of a song on the hallowed grounds of Grassroots. This summer love would last and grow more beautiful by the day. They decided in their young hearts and old souls to travel this journey towards Leyla's death together, and journey they did. It was transcendent and kind. Frida Kahlo wrote "take a lover who looks at you like maybe you are magic." This is the gift that Jared gave to Leyla in each moment.

JAMON Julia's partner. Joined the family early 2014, he's the love of Julia's life and high school sweetheart. He re-oriented their lives at an achingly difficult time, bringing her love, beauty and hope in the dark days. Father extraordinaire, firefighter, personal trainer, and anything sports-ball enthusiast. He once showed up at Hospice after working on a water main break; it was like 12 degrees in late February and he had been soaking wet. His arrival that morning, dry and sans fire truck, marked the emergence of our death watch. He brought bourbon to fuel our Glad Game. Smart man.

JASMIN Jessica's best friend, Katherine and Melissa's mother. Our very own manifestation of the fountain of youth, she reverse-ages each year, and somehow we love her for it. I was once asked at the advanced age of 21 if she were my daughter. Jasmin has hosted more sleepovers for Melissa, Leyla, and Amy than there are nights in a year. She should get an award for long, patient, conversations lasting into the early hours of morning.

Deeply listening to each and every teenage thought without judgment, giving only simple and gentle guidance.

JEFF Leyla's therapist and Spiritual Friend, the universe mixed up something delightful when he manifested in this lifelifetime. A laughing Buddha, spiritual ninja, right heart hugging, walking poet, and sitting man of sunshine, he helped Leyla know her true self and the delicious perfection of her infinite being. He cleared the forest, so that Leyla could find the path and follow the voice of the Great Mother calling her home.

JEFF FOOTE Our official Village photographer, he captured so many of the beautiful shots within these pages as well as the rear cover photo. We love him endlessly for telling our story in pictures.

JESSICA JONES [Written by our Katie] Amy's twin, Mama Zen Bear, founder of Leyla's Village, writer and narrator. Weaving tales and lassoing soul-deep feelings, transforming them into a painting of words. The magical queen of our hearts, she dances salsa in stiletto heels under the wolf moon. She drinks beneath the stars…meadow-tea in her left hand and wine in her right. She is dressed in hummingbirds gathering nectar from turquoise and indigo blossoms. Of our solstice twins, she is the balancer; the producer of practical, intelligent purpose and passion-filled spiritual dreams in a single

breath. She is devotion in action, a do-er and a dreamer. A mother of mothers, she is an abundance of beauty tucked under a warm shawl. Upon emerging from her nest, she scatters the love of this Hive like sunflower seeds, and cultivates the blossom of our sweet girl's story for our Village, who loves her ever so big.

JESSICA SNYDER Leyla's "Jessibee" and Mountain Jam companion, Jessica has a funky, beautiful heart that Leyla could see for miles. They shared a love of retro clothes and one another.

JULIA aka Jukes, aka Momma, aka Universal Feeding Machine, Blissful Dying heroine, mother of Leyla, and many years later Opal, Esmae, Violet, Tahjay, and Aysia. Master task-er, likes her man hot, but not on fire, and her martinis dirty. Our Julia has learned through the most profound experiences that there is joy in suffering. Even in the shit-storm of life, there is a glimmer of hope just around the bend, and this trodden path most likely leads to a sunny, flower-filled meadow.

KAT (Katherine) Melissa's older sister, the oldest of the big kids, Katherine got to call all of the shots, because, well, she was clearly the coolest. She made up their little kid games, while Melissa, Leyla and Michael eagerly followed along. She ruled the catwalk and had the best dance steps, while Melissa and Leyla were rappers and Michael an MC.

KATIE Julia's sister and Leyla's aunt, she was Leyla's other mother, coaching her from the womb and into the world. Leyla had a second home with our Katie who always maintained a bedroom for Leyla in her home and a place inside the center of her heart. Our Katie loves, loves, loves her people. Fiercely devoted, she loses herself in the wonder of consignment shops, her arms full of little treasures she gives away. She spends each summer day in Nature's church- a wide open farmland CSA where she finds the beauty of God ever present in the growing kale and wild flowers.

KATHLEEN *see Nonni

LESLIE Papa's sister and Julia and Katie's aunt. A treasure hunter, history keeper, book fairy and thrifter of anything from a good loaf of bread to a classic car. Our dainty, practical and loving auntie shared her born day with our Leyla, so there were always extra cakes, and wishes floating by.

LINDA Dietrich family friend since before time. She is always close and easy to spot in her red convertible. Violet thinks Dos Equis should have her on commercials because even though Linda does not imbibe, she is unequivocally "the most interesting woman in the world!" Also, she has really, really cool hair.

MAE Jamon's mother, grandmother to Jamon and Julia's children. Oh our Miss Mae, with her tiny dog and her fabulous stories about using a hot iron heated with flames to straighten hair. All the while, spinning around for hugs, and giving us her bright smile and lighting up our hearts with her laughter.

MARLEY Jared's sister, friend of Leyla. A free spirit, mountain hiker, farmer's market enthusiast she is sprinkling our Village love all over the South. Marley once made a mad dash home during the fall semester, in a blizzard, to lay eyes on Leyla and snuggle her close before she undertook her final journey.

MELI/MELISSA Leyla's best friend, 1/3 of Leyla's whole. Cousins who shapeshifted into friends and then sisters and then into sleeping mermaids with their long, black hair intertwined, and their limbs twisted together like crawling, flower-full vines. Melissa, ever full of silly-amplified, is a fountain of laughter that makes us roll our eyes, and find our own laughter bubbling to the surface. Melissa makes our love-burst happy and light of heart, a twinkling glow.

MELYNDA friend of Julia, Village do-er. Believes that the cure to any ailment lives inside the goodness of coconut oil, she will publicly shame her loved ones to prevent them from eating anything not organic or locally-sourced from a biodiverse, guru-farmer. Once went to McDonald's to fulfill a desperate Julia's Hospice craving, which might nominate her for some kind of awesome award.

MICHAEL Jessica's son, Leyla's cousin and personal-security. Michel was our firstborn and saw Leyla as his little sister. They shared years of a communal style living as Amy, Julia and I lived a stone's throw from one another. Three mothers and two children with open doors and fridges. They shared endless sleepovers, actual live pets, stuffed animals, and probably dirty socks. For once, Michael followed instructions exactly, and acted as the bouncer at Leyla's calling hours at Corks and More.

MODEL CITIZEN TATTOO The official tattoo shop of Leyla's Village owned by our very own ink master James Spiers. Between James and Phoebe they have tattooed the L4 stories that rest in our heart in ink under our skin, decorating our bodies with our most precious mantra.

MY PAPA aka Rick Rogers. Encountered the fountain of youth in Ithaca Beer Company's Pale Ale and has not aged a day in the last 15 years. Editor-at-large, hater of any metaphor involving wombs and bears.

NANA aka Deb Dietrich, Julia and Katie's mother and Leyla's grandmother. Our original gypsy who finds peace deep in jungles, rainforests and sandy beaches. A fierce and loving warrior, she taught us that it is never a good idea to stand between a mother and her babies, as you might, A. get warned, and B. get run over. Just for fun, she also shows us that sewing a cape, while knitting warm mittens, making tiramisu, and having a career is actually possible. She ultimately allows us to understand that she is the mother of Superwomen everywhere. Nana would stop the Whole World to fulfill Leyla's wishes with a forceful "just go ahead and push my I don't give a SHIT button."

NONNI aka. Kathleen, Rich's mother and Katie's mother in law. As soft as the wind and gentle as a feather. She treads lightly on this earth and has her own sphere of love that is wide enough to encompass us all. We are fairly certain she amplifies our own goodness in the world, and raises our group average. Leyla's Village shines brightly into the vastness with her in our lives.

NONNO aka Rick, Rich's father and Katie's father in law. A gentle giant and official captain of the boat that Leyla so loved. She would sit and rock on the gentle waves and leap into the slippery world of water and joy. Rick is a mushroom whisperer and giver of life. Throughout Leyla's illness he was a magical procurer of the elusive and healing

Turkey Tail, and My Community mushrooms. After Leyla's death he and Rich spent untold hours making an urn for Leyla's bones to rest. Over 600 pieces of wood, from all over the world, and beautiful turquoise-every single tiny piece crafted with love. I still weep every time I think of its beauty.

OPAL Leyla's sister and muse, Julia's second daughter. Once went with her pals Emma and Sophie to an upscale restaurant, where they ordered water with fruit, and four mozzarella sticks. It should be noted, they had no money and no plan. Opal, with her diamond exterior and the softest of insides, she is a tiger in all things, as fierce as Leyla was gentle. This journey, this book, is about our Opal; it is the living, breathing, manifestation of Leyla's loving her beyond a place called death. In the unfolding of Opal's life, she has grown into Leyla's sunflower.

PAPA aka Timmy Dietrich, Julia and Katie's father, Leyla's grandfather and great love. He greets the world and his people with "hey, yo!" A real-life master of Zen and motorcycles, he is a wide-porch dwelling, flower-picking, guitar-strumming, vacation-crashing, man of walking heart. In our times of unsteadiness, the predictability of his arrival to fetch compost, and state the obvious "God damn it, this sucks," has a profoundly centering quality. For these reasons, he was the best Leyla-rocker of all times.

PAUL Ali's fiancé and Waylon's father. Man of big trucks and excavators, took his son on his first tractor ride when he was only a few days old. Now, child and dog are competition for official co-pilot status.

RICH Katie's husband and Leyla's uncle. Man of quilts-piled-high, he tucked our Leyla in on so many nights that this ritual had a sort of magic that made her believe he pulled a blanket of stars to cover her in the brilliant night sky. Rich and Leyla were peas in a pod, and toward the end of Leyla's life, Rich gently carried her home for one last sleepover. In the final days at Hospice, amid laughter and thrown Alaskan Shearling boots, he tucked quilts, fluffed pillows, and made sure his Leyla had everything her heart desired. He always brought the starry sky with him-it is just how he rolls.

RICK* see Nonno

ROB Amy's husband. Might be at this moment explaining to one of the little ones why sugar is poison and that a smoothie with kale is a much more delicious option than birthday cake. He is likely cooking at the stove AND talking with Melynda about food conspiracies.

SADIE Leyla's dog who died. She was tiny, and easy to wash in the sink, though giving her a haircut brought out a much bigger dog, with much bigger teeth.

SHANA Julia's best friend. Our wild child, outer space costume diva, she may show up in our driveway at any given moment, after deciding to take a quick 5 hour road trip just to lay her eyes on her people. She once was the unwitting participant in a Hospice peep show attraction starring a bathroom, a shower debacle, and Stevie Wonder radio. In our desire to bathe our girl bright and clean, Shana and I climbed naked into a shower stall with Leyla. In our infinite wisdom, we hung Leyla's call-button necklace around Shana's neck. Our sassy little mischievous girl chose to invite others to our shower-fest and pressed the call button for assistance we did not need at all. As a result, there is many a nurse that have seen us in full glory.

SOPHIE Amy's youngest, our daughter of untamed hair and dancing feet, at her advanced age, she has more rhythm than all of us. She can rock out hip hop, salsa, and bachata all while standing in the kitchen waiting for dinner. Sophie is our original groupie, following Papa around at Bethany Beach asking sweetly for him to play his guitar for her. She probably busted out a flamenco dance, though I may have made that part up.

SPENCER Jessica's husband. Was unavailable for comment as he travels often for work. When home he can usually be found painting, baking delicious bread, hanging ceiling fans, building rooms in Julia's basement. When he is not making an obscene amount of racket, he is usually hunting AND being bitten by a tick.

STELLA Katie's oldest daughter, cousin to Leyla. Our bell-bottomed hippie-child, as kind and gentle as a woodland nymph. Stella and Leyla snuggled in for more story times than there are words in this book. They shared the same love of a cozy bed, a place for snuggling in under handmade quilts and sleeping long within bedrooms that expressed their similar eclectic style and love of nature's elements.

TAJ/TAHJAY Jamon's oldest child. Experienced being a younger sibling for such a short time, and loved every minute. Taj is our resident actor, a creative, free-spirit, who uses words that often require that we have a dictionary on hand. Taj is like a snow leopard, very elusive and is sure to be on the set of a play somewhere.

VIOLET Julia's daughter, the older of the twins. Our sweetly demanding little Violet, she moves through the world seriously. In her delightful intensity, she bathed us in hope and lightened our hearts. She and her sister were born of the sort of magic where we came to know love not only lived, it grew in us. Violet one ½ of the superhero team of little savior-ettes.

WAYLON Ali and Paul's son, a blond haired, blue eyed angel face, though he was very young at the time, Ali's pregnancy and Waylon's arrival of his perfect little baby-self gave us many miles of happiness and delight.

the hive

Leyla wrote of her own journey...

I stand here, in this rainstorm, and somehow the sunshine still finds a way to warm my skin. No rain storm can take away my love of life.

My diagnosis has given me a deeper knowing. Something tells me that something good will come out of this. In fact, my illness has been a gift to me. I have been able to find who I really am, and why I was placed here.

This book is to share with you my hardships and my small victories. And to show you that maybe, just maybe, by the end of these words, you can stand in the rain and still feel the sun.

blissful dying

leyla wrote of her own journey...

Will you stay a while longer, my daughter, my sister, my friend?
So that you may see that I carry you with me
in each passing heartbeat for all of
my remaining days.
Carry with you my infinite and joyful love,
it is yours to take when you leave.
I will meet you in the Great Beyond
where I will love you still,
with each passing heartbeat.

—Love, Jessi

blissful dying

In the Beginning

Leyla was the first of my daughters, the rosy Buddha child born of my sister-friend, Julia.
For much of my childhood, and all of my todays since, Julia, and her older sister, Katie, have
inhabited the world I share with my identical twin, Amy. There were street fights and dance-offs,
runaways and wide porches, shared vegetable gardens and Christmas trees with roots and dirt
disguised as ornaments. There were diner interventions and Volvos with bass and winding roads
named "a million ways to die." There were baby brothers at sweet 16, terrible fast food jobs, and
a mother who died too young in a living room bathed in the rising sun.

There was Guatemala, of course, and Mexico, which is better left untold. There were new
adventures, and sisters who follow, to keep what is sacred close at heart. There were motorcycles
and apple trees, and juke boxes that we might have forced into retirement. There were old dogs
who rocked dreads and chased us in the dark, their mouths full of deer bones, and a horse with a
questionable end, and pot roasts which were totally unrelated to horse.

There were sweet grandparents and delicious pancakes and city busses full of freedom,
and at least a billion astoundingly bad choices, and one criminal impersonation. We are blessed

with a giant life, and built a love nest for
the wooly mammoth heart; a place where
friendships are born.

When our Leyla was diagnosed with
inoperable brain cancer in the summer of
2012 just after her Quinceañera, our world
came to a full and paralyzing halt. After
days in different hospitals, Leyla and Julia
came home to the saddest and stupidest of
all homecoming parties. Leyla wrapped her
arms around her sobbing mama, who had
the air hunger of a woman who had been
formally introduced to the edgeless nature
of panic. I was helpless to mute their pain,
and desperate. Leyla's Village was born that
afternoon out of this profound and honest
desperation and the belief that suffering
comes from the same place as joy and love

and hope. It was born of the belief that kindness has a way of untangling sorrow, and that a broken heart creates more space for the deliciousness of the world to crawl in.

What started as a way to ease life for Julia and Leyla, to coordinate meals, and chemotherapy chauffeurs, morphed into a story, one we can all recognize because it is our own, and so utterly human. I wrote updates to the village with the gift of Julia's and Leyla's trust, and shared the bone crushing truth of their lives dissected. This village we love to distraction is a living, breathing organism, and a metaphor for the beauty of belonging; it is the love bubble where we rest our hearts. Our origins run along a deeper, longer course, for we were a village long before Leyla's Village, only we did not have a name or fully recognize our purpose. Julia wrote our village creation story once, and it went like this...

• •

Our village was founded by mothers. Our Founding Mothers were those who drank too much Chardonnay at baby showers, polar plunged, pursued dreams of going back to college repeatedly, welcomed one another's children in our homes when need be, sometimes in the middle of the night. We cooked elaborate group dinners, danced, lit bonfires, braved new cities, took chances. We threw chemo parties. Our mothers survived and succumbed to breast cancer. We organized parties, brunches, and benefits; travelled the world, gypsy feet. We documented our journey. We learned hard lessons in love, sometimes more than twice. We bore witness to suffering, we listened to one another's stories without judgement. We loved each other fiercely. We survived. We are survivors, all of us, even Leyla, who survived a series of life's greatest challenges and tribulations. She flourished with grace, patience, love, humility, hilarity, and bliss. She knew that time was all she had. She used her life to its full potential. We taught her well, all of us, the Founding Mothers...

• •

Leyla, knowing her time was waning, wanted to share the truth of her life. We began writing her story together, a natural evolution; as I had been narrating and sharing her world from deep inside the hive from the beginning. Leyla wanted to leave her family with a reflection of sorts; something to shine brightly for her clan after her death. She called this work Blissful Dying, and asked that I publish it after the story of her life and death had been written. This was our secret, the best and only one I ever kept. As Leyla's time grew shorter she changed her mind about Blissful, she wanted to see her family and friends soak in its beauty. So then we wrote furiously and without mind to grammar, or actual words, or any curfews.

Leyla delighted her family and our clan with this labor of love. We imprinted her photographs deep in our eyes and ate her memories and words so they could rest on our insides. Leyla wanted her experience to help people live better lives, to find gratitude even when the sky fell onto the earth and lay broken and weeping in our laps; to stand in the

blissful dying

center of a rainstorm and feel the kiss of the warm sunshine. She wanted this to be her legacy, a way she could touch us long after she left…we are halfway to the truth.

The rest of *Blissful Dying* was written in the darkness of winter, under a mountain of snow and hand sewn quilts; and ends with death and hope and humility. We hope that this book will inspire others to hunt laughter and meaning like it is a hidden treasure, to look for it behind trees, and inside kangaroo pockets, to let its goodness rest deeply in the heart's center. We hope that it will remind us to pause, to be here now, to breathe action into intention, and to smile like it matters. We hope that you will read this and recognize that your own journey is reflected in what has been written; and that you will come to find it achingly beautiful and full of who you truly are. We hope that it will touch anyone who seeks to find the place where finite and infinity, meet and fall in love.

Big love,

Jessica

• •
We hope that this deeply entangled beautiful mess will reflect you, and you, and you; and that we will come to recognize this humanness in one another.
• •

OCTOBER 22, 2012
The Land of Ron

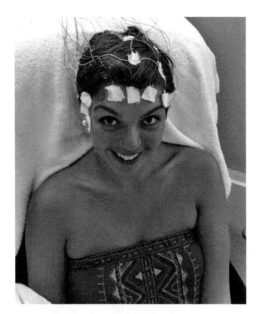

Today we are all breathing a great sigh of relief as Leyla finished her radiation treatment today, and on Julia's birthday nonetheless—what a sweet gift to unwrap. These last six weeks have conjured up a wide array of emotions and experiences. When Leyla began her radiation treatment she traveled the first few days back and forth to Rochester, a 5-hour roundtrip for a 30 minute appointment. It became clear in the early days that the trip was just too exhausting for her and so, during the week, Leyla and Julia would pack up and move away from home.

The continuous coordinating for Leyla's 6-year-old sister Opal was anxiety producing and complex. We were fully aware that she needed huge doses of extra love and also a deep rootedness and grounding in routine. Not only was her Momma gone, but Leyla as well. We stuffed Julia's home with loving mamas who knew Opal best and who showered her with extra layers of emotional fortitude, and probably some sweet spoiling as well. Most times we floated along this trajectory just fine, until Opal would melt into a puddle because she demanded to wear her tutu to school or refused to go at all. Fortunately, your status as a mother is not stripped from you if your child goes to school in a tutu, or not having brushed her teeth, or god forbid without her hair brushed. We were honest with ourselves and others that Opal's emotional safety was what we were striving for, and anything else was really just shit in comparison.

In Rochester land, things were a bit sunnier, as Leyla and Julia would drive out Monday mornings full of Ithaca Bakery breakfast and hot chocolate and coffee to go. After radiation they would settle in at Ron's House (Ronald McDonald), and snuggle up in their room and watch

22

blissful dying

Netflix on their IPad's tiny screen. They fell into a bridal TV show marathon, which has outlived even the radiation course and has a similar side effect of nausea for those of us who have to listen to this great passion of theirs.

While Leyla and Julia were a bit like exiled strangers in Ron's Land, it was also a wonderful time for them to just soak in one another. There were lots of dinners out, shopping trips and walks along Ontario beach, and visits with our Rochester contingent. In these early days the emotionality of their lives had tipped on its axis and we held close an abiding promise that time would begin to heal that wound. It was as if laughter and joy had become something of a taboo…and any lightness of heart would be immediately followed by deeply wrenching guilt and ultimately, profound sadness, particularly for Julia. This exile gave our girls time to settle into their new lives, one full of cancer and hope that they would be able to steal just a little more time.

On Thursday nights, Nana would drive to Rochester and settle in with Leyla, and Julia would head for home. Since Opal is with her Dad on Thursday nights there was never a reason to rush back to Ithaca. Ever wondering where my friend was and curious for updates on her whereabouts, I asked her what delayed her so. Over tea Julia described an ever present aching that rested deep in her heart, which made her throat lumpy and her breath come at a price. She told me that getting into the car and driving aimlessly in the general direction of home was just one of the ways to let their new life settle inside of her mind.

So, my friend would get lost on purpose, taking left turn after left turn, just to see what there was to find on her detoured path home in the darkness.

And after this latest journey of living and leaving and coming home, Leyla is settled in with her Katie and Rich for a quiet slumber party. The rest of us opted to sit in our gratitude and our togetherness under this chilly, fall moon, and soak in the crisp dark air full of wine. Papa dropped in as we were readying ourselves for Julia's birthday dinner at Northstar. He declined our invitation to join us claiming that it was a "femfest," and wished us a fabulous time. We found later that night at Northstar, our bellies full of tapas and cheesecake and laughter that something had shifted in the night, for the edgeless quality of panic, guilt, and aching opened slightly to a new remembering; the remembering of joy.

Big Love,

Jessica

A Couch Love Affair

We love you more today than we did yesterday, which almost seems impossible because we already love you biggest of all.

We are still reeling from the magic you spun in darkness at the Love for Leyla benefit. The delight of each of you piled on top of the surprise appearance of Trumansburg Takes on Pediatric Cancer and Make a Wish Foundation left me speechless, which is very hard to do. We are cherishing each of your words, and the memory of your beautiful faces and how it felt to be blessed with your gifts of kindness and love. Your deliciousness is the beating heart of Leyla's Village. Thank you.

Last night we found ourselves so easily falling into the beautiful music, the rhythm of dancing, and the shiny shaved heads of our Leyla, and my Amy, who looked like beautiful crystal balls of wonder. My Amy shaved her head only weeks ago, wanting to show Leyla the way to her inner beauty, and to teach all of our little girls that beauty resides on our insides and shines its way outside to decorate these bodies we put on each morning. Our sweet Leyla, in her easy grace chose this event to show off her new style, and was, as always, radiant.

We are so grateful that Leyla's chemotherapy treatment had been postponed and that she was chemotherapy free during her celebration. She felt so wonderfully well, full to bursting with her abundant store of harvested sunshine. What a gift it was to her to feel truly well in her body and light of heart. Chemotherapy appointment cancellations are lovely, little miracles sent from the land of divine intervention.

Now Leyla is on an additional oral chemotherapy drug five days out of each month,

blissful dying

and it has truly extracted all of our sweet girl's precious reserves. Our baby is super ill, and all we can do is hold her gently in our laps, careful not to move or shift in our skin. We speak in hushed tones, so as not to wake the beastly searing of the brain. We rub lavender on her pulses and temples and above her closed eyes. We brew chamomile and mint tea, and offer her tiny mouthfuls like a waiting baby bird. We pile up on couches with Shana, who has come home to nest, a perfect concoction for a couch fest. It has been a time for channeling the inner sloth, and covering up with comfy blankets. So this week, the couch won.

We find it difficult to accept that in order for Leyla to live a stronger healthier life, she may have to feel truly horrible first. In these painful, achingly nauseous times we have learned that when we fold ourselves together, this dark crossroad we must travel beyond is subtly brighter, more bearable. So we climb into our love bubble and we rest our hearts here. Being together in this place makes our scary and dark more cozy, more luminous. We are glow bugs in love bubble, shining bright- readying our Leyla for a beautiful metamorphosis.

We are traveling onwards in time to a new day and a new week. There have been Christmas trees to decorate and elves to find. Leyla is enjoying the view of these festivities from sloth land, and whenever able, joins in for whatever precious moments she can.

As Thanksgiving fades into the not so distant past I offer one final thought of thanks to you. Leyla's Village has taught me that love is not finite and tangible, but expansive, infinite, and transformative. Leyla's Village is a thing of beauty.

Big Love,

Jessica

a couch love affair

Midnight Magic

There is much aflutter as we greet the snows of early winter, so let us pause together and reflect on all that is. Leyla and Julia went to their old stomping grounds in DC to celebrate New Year's with Shana. They had a wonderful time and the two of them were positively glowing with life. They had a posh suite downtown, new dresses for wearing, and a more pressing urgency than most to make this New Year's count. While many of us were deep in slumber at midnight, Jukes, Leyla and Shana were enjoying a champagne toast at La Tasca, with all the love and excitement of ushering in a new beginning. This brief trip was the sort of rejuvenation magic that is so vital when our illusions are shattered irreparably.

We are profoundly grateful that Leyla has been feeling well. She has intentionally created space in her life to ponder some really hard questions, ones that sadly have no easy answers. Leyla is learning so much about herself and is struggling to find the balance of it all. The idea of school and all of the new frustrations she has encountered as her brain and cognition change so rapidly, contrasted with the finite moments in which she has to live them, has become so very real. It is clear that some people live their whole lives and rest in old age, having never faced the question of their own mortality and the meaning of their own existence. Leyla is working with Jeff, an amazing and tender therapist and spiritual friend who is helping her to cultivate an organic conversation, full of the possibility of dying in a manner that is full of living.

Leyla has been very clear that her life is not, and will not ever be reduced to endurance and survival; but rather that her life is about thriving and living and loving and hope. I have many favorite sayings that I have heard over the years that I carry with me, and one in particular has begun to creep into my mind whenever I think of Leyla. Mother Teresa said, "May God break my heart so completely that the whole world falls in."

Leyla's heart is painfully wide and open, her gracefulness and beauty shines even in the muddiest of

· ·

To want to embrace all the suffering that the world has to offer, and create love, compassion, and understanding from such brokenness is a gift for those soulful few who have the depth and grace of spirit to derive deep and abiding wisdom from the raw, unvarnished truth of our existence.

· ·

puddles. Perhaps we can learn from her, and allow our hearts to become a little more fragile, a little more open. Perhaps in doing so, we can invite ourselves to our very own conversation about seeking the courage to live an authentic life. Onwards to Puerto Rico, where limos await, the sun is always sunny and even the mud puddles are giant, glorious, playgrounds.

Big Love,

Jessica

The Beach of Crazy Horse

Last week, Leyla's Papa, feeling a bit left out of all things Make a Wish trip mentioned his desire to go with Leyla to Puerto Rico. Leyla jumped all over the opportunity to convince him that he just had to go. She didn't exactly have to beg… Papa packed his bags (I am sure he did not have to agonize over what to pack), booked a flight and met Julia, Leyla, Opal and Nana at the resort on Saturday.

Julia, Leyla, Opal and Nana flew out last Thursday morning and were picked up by a stretch limo just as Opal's bus was passing the house, with all of Opal's friends on it. Little Miss Opal loves all things swank and is sure to get a lot of mileage out of that one at school. In the airport, Nana having worn shoes with a platform heel, remarked at her odd choice, commenting to Opal, that she was not sure how she was going to manage to walk in them. In my all-time favorite Opal-isim she told Nana in her sassiest voice "Well Nana, you gon' learn to-day, you gon' learn to-day." I almost can't write the rest of this story, I am still laughing so hard.

Once in Puerto Rico, the family totally dug into sun and fun. Eating pulpo (octopus), going to the El Yunque rainforest and heading off the beaten path as Nana and Papa are wont to do. They sought the downtown vibe to fill themselves with non-tourist experiences, enjoying local Luquillo beach, sampling delicious food from street vendors and taking in local shops. They relaxed, played in the sand, and lived a foodie's dream.

Leyla fell in love with kayaking at night across Bioluminescent Bay, with only the moonlight and her mother for company. I can see her in my mind's eye paddling across a wide expanse of beautiful iridescent ocean in darkness with only the subdued light of a full moon to light the way. She described the utter tranquility, and indescribable beauty of it all. Not every adventure on the trip was rosy. There was, in fact, a horseback riding excursion on the beach that was, shall we say -alarming. Leyla and her Papa went on a

blissful dying

ride; after all, when Katie, Julia, Amy and I were growing up, Papa had a horse. Having met at least one horse in his life, he was experienced. He was not afraid. He is an earthy, go with the flow kind of fella who rides a big motorcycle … need I say more? Our Leyla was a bit petrified, the horses were not super gentle. In fact, this was an excursion that just might have warranted a bit of experience, or perhaps skill. Timmy had a horse that just surely was going to throw him off, with the horse standing on his hind legs and such. Not so relaxing, not so calm, however, they did survive and I, for one, enjoyed how Julia relayed the terror from her astute observer's standpoint. So my friends, that's a wrap for the trip.

Moving forward, Leyla is getting settled back into her life at home. As I mentioned recently, Leyla has been struggling with some difficult questions. She has difficulty connecting at school emotionally and cognitively. She is struggling with not learning at the rate of her friends and peers. In her worst times she feels, well "stupid." So, this week Leyla will begin the process of incorporating a tutor into her life at home and leave the adventure and the stress of traditional school for another, healthier time or not at all. We are so delighted by this decision and simply know that the learning she is doing in her life is so much greater than what she will learn staring at a blackboard in a classroom. This is a better choice for Leyla. Anything that we can do to help reduce the stress and increase the amount of well-being for Leyla will be done. Hopefully, through these loving efforts she can do the real work of living her life to the fullest. We always seem to mix the wonderful with the weighty in our musings together. But truly, perhaps this is the way it is supposed to be- a true path along the middle way.

Big Love,

Jessica

the beach of crazy horse

Letter From A Village

Dr. Korones,

I am writing to you on behalf of Leyla's Village, a group of loving and committed family, friends, and community members of a patient of yours, Miss Leyla Dietrich. Leyla mentioned that there may be an opportunity for you to provide a recommendation for her to join a group of other young people with cancer that will travel to Florida together. I am writing to you on behalf of her village in the deepest hope that this opportunity may become a reality for her. Perhaps this letter may help the organization hosting this trip get to know a little about Leyla, and what she might contribute to such an event.

When Leyla was diagnosed with a brain tumor late last summer we were collectively saddened, devastated and deeply shaken from the news. I joined Leyla and her mother Julia, on their front porch as they sat and cried together their first day home. Leyla let quiet tears fall, as she wrapped her arms around her mother who was quite frankly, undone.

That day, feeling utterly helpless, I decided to do the only thing I could for Leyla and Julia and that was to create Leyla's Village; a place where people could connect to get news, provide love and support, and offer kindnesses small and large. Leyla's Village is a passionate group devoted to helping Leyla heal, abide the toughest treatments with grace and live the most extraordinary of lives for as long as the universe allows.

Late summer, last year a group of women got together to plan a small benefit and gathering for Leyla. We were not only interested in helping offset the cost of hospital stays, travel back and forth to Rochester but also, and perhaps most importantly, to provide an opportunity for Leyla to be affirmed by the love of close friends and family. We wanted her to see with her own eyes, the innate power she had to bring people together. We were completely unprepared for the unfolding of this event. The people who came from near and far, the bands who played, the local restaurant that hosted and the sheer positivity of it all was more profound than any single experience I have had in my life.

You see, this was not a small affair of close family and friends, but a giant outpouring of support from everyone who has been touched by Leyla. Leyla loved her party, and in her brave and fearless way she went for the first time in public, with her recently shaven head, shiny and bright for all the world to see. We have all learned so much from her astounding inner beauty and deep humility.

While Leyla has an amazing and fully natural capacity to empathize with others, we have found ourselves profoundly lacking in the experience to empathize with her. While many of us would gladly throw in our lot to take her place, we are frustratingly unable. And though many of us have loved and lost, suffered terrible tragedy and illnesses; this seems altogether different. Facing a terminal illness of a child is a soul shifting, life altering experience. As a village, we come to Leyla with older eyes, with life experiences that were shaped mostly and gratefully over time. While we sometimes ask ourselves the same questions, like "does it hurt to die", our musings and the attitude with which we approach this is altogether different-because we have had time on our side.

Leyla is the most astounding young woman I have ever met or known. Her abundant optimism, kindness and generosity of spirit and self simply makes the world a better place.

We would like to make Leyla's world a better place too. We want her to have the opportunity to experience her illness and the treatment process with people who can see through her eyes, who have similar questions and similar hope for their future. Please submit this with your recommendation for Leyla if you think it will help her chances to join this special group of young people. And thank you, thank you, thank you, for the care, expertise and compassion that you bring to Leyla's treatment.

— Jessica, writing on behalf of Leyla's Village

letter from a village

Rainstorm

Sickness
Me
Changed my world
Looking differently
So differently
Do you?
I'm leaving
Not yet
And God ain't fixin anything
Breathing in
And out
Cool rain hitting my palms
While people run for cover
I stop
I stand
I feel
I am alive
Take a minute
Feel life
Think of those
who know they're leaving
Do you stop?
Do you stand?
Do you feel?
You're alive

blissful dying

I love you, and you, and you

It has been an amazing and travel-filled Spring: Florida, New Orleans, Bethany Beach and beyond...the travel was a deep learning experience for Leyla. While some nurtured her curious, gypsy soul she also found a deep longing for family, place and home.

Bethany beach was an extra special trip. Leyla was joined by her whole extended family including the Cacciotti women, the DeAugistine-Jones and Stone clan, and our lovely ladies, Miss Shana and Amy C. We had an amazing time with the brilliant, curious and playful girls, our "sandwich" generation of mothers and aunts, and our parents. Papa played the guitar to our clan and was followed everywhere with said guitar by a sweetly devoted 6-year-old Sophie. Little Augie played in the sand, and the ocean...well, the ocean saw all of us. The girls boogie boarded endlessly, and played sweetly, covered in sand like little ocean nymphs. There was pickle ball played on the burning sand, date nights, boardwalk strolling and a slightly hideous promise executed so that all the girls could go to Fun-Land. It is the official land of sensory overload- a place of screaming children, bumper cars, and the ping ping siren of festival games. The kids were devastated at leaving the land of fun, and the rest of us just passed around the Advil and gave thanks to all things silent.

On a sunny, late Sunday afternoon Leyla was surprised with a, wait for it, wait for it...a shiny sapphire blue convertible VW BUG!!! She danced, and we all laughed and were joyful with her. We danced in the street like absolutely no one was watching, to the pumping stereo of the stationary car. This most elegant gift was from an inspiring and much loved man, Leyla's late grandfather, Dr. Webb Fiser.

We were all stunned and amazed by my Amy's utter creativity as the L4 symbol and mantra "Live Life Like Leyla" shimmered into her mind and out of her mouth on the sandy street. She later reflected it was a most excellent use of her tuition dollars and recent statistics course that had plagued her so. And stealing exponents is right up my Amy's alley, so there was that to be oddly grateful for. We floated on our new mantra and the breeze soaking up our beachy time, wrapping it up by honoring the Super Moon in true worship fashion. Leyla, Amy C. and me, with the assistance of Michael AKA-clothing rack...swam at twilight enfolded deeply in the ocean waves. This was a blissful and once in a lifetime moment, and we were delighted by our good fortune as we were not even munched on a little bit by sharks at feeding time. Defying the odds, that's how we roll.

Fast forward to present day- Grassroots Music Festival is in our rear view mirror where Leyla could be found dancing to Donna the Buffalo, The Gun Poets and The Blind Spots with her sweet boy, Jared. She is, at a glance, a teenager living a normal life, filled with friends, boys, travel, family and dreams. We know her to be thoughtful, and beyond her experience in years. Leyla brings her old soul to her young life, possessing wisdom and grace that we don't quite yet grasp...

Leyla was proudly registered as a "survivor" in the most recent Relay for Life event in Ithaca. She is so young to be a survivor and we dream of a world where we may all live to be old survivors, though we know this will never come to pass...Leyla had her most recent MRI last week and while there are no reports of growth, there are also no distinct signs of the tumor shrinking. It is a wait and see game and Leyla is mindfully weighing her future options.

And so, we entered birthday land, so grateful that Leyla made it to her sweet 16. Shana surprised us with a visit, telling no one, simply showing up in the driveway with a vision of Leyla in her heart and an utter determination to hold her baby tight on her birthing day. The day was beautiful and chilly for August, with a sky full of sunshine and puffy white clouds. It was the kind of day where one is content to lay in the grass and sky gaze; which of course is exactly what we did.

We had her birthday bash at her Papa's house with our whole clan. We filled our arms with the beauty of one another and our bellies with amazing seafood,

blissful dying

salads, gumbo and cheese grits. The younger kids climbed trees, dazzled us with gymnastics on the lawn and snuggled in for quick hugs from grown-ups before darting away again. Leyla snuggled into the porch swing and rocked with Amy C. and Melissa, back and forth in a swing that feels so perfectly comfortable because it has all of the stored love of friends it has rocked through the ages.

It was one of those days where you want to simply take a deep breath, find your place in the world, and root yourself firmly in your gratitude and bottle the joy. Laughter, music, magic balloons that traveled through space and time, and a giant old gingerbread man candle were witness to Leyla's birthday wish. Big love, that is what this life is about after all, and the singular reason to wake us each day to this delicious, blessed life.

We have truly awakened to the precious gift of birthdays, for they are beautiful measurements of our life journey. Julia shared a Japanese proverb with me this morning that seems to resonate with this heartbreaking journey; "things are most beautiful when they are dying." To breathe through this most humbling truth and find laughter, love, and meaning is a grace I pray that we all possess. Bottle your bliss sweet friends, and cherish it for another day.

Big Love,

Jessica

Big Hearts and Woven Baskets

My Katie,

"Hush, little baby, don't say a word. Your Katie's gonna buy you a mockingbird." I remember falling asleep to you singing this song to me. You are my Katie. You taught me how to be a beach baby. We share a deep love for the ocean, and when my toes are in the sand I can't help but think of you. So many weekly sleepovers and trips to Taughannock with a picnic basket full of treats. I love you so, so very much.

" I love you! "

Rich,

You are the best thing that has happened to this family. I feel like I have known you forever and am so grateful. I have loved watching our families come together, like it was always meant to be this way. My simple, yet incredible highlights. Boat days, movie nights, watching Augie have too much frozen yogurt, which resulted in endless spinning and running and jumping and laughing. The first time I met you was the first moment I saw Katie falling in love. Thank you for being you, Rich, and for sharing your family with ours. You have a golden heart. You, simply, are the best uncle I could ask for.

Courtesy of Jeffrey Foote Photography

blissful dying

Change Is...

The end of summer always brings change, our sunny days begin to diminish and our autumn this year has seemed to arrive particularly early. Last week was particularly difficult for Leyla and her entire extended family and friends. Sadie, Leyla's 1½ year old puppy was attacked by two pit bulls who broke through the 5 foot fence separating Julia's property from that of their owners. While Julia and Amy were at Taughannock Falls with the little girls, Leyla watched as the horror of the attack unfolded. We are deeply grateful for two things. The first, is that Leyla's boyfriend Jared was there and ran out to protect Sadie from further attack. The second, and the source of our deepest and most profound gratitude, is that neither Leyla nor Jared were attacked in the process of rescuing Sadie.

Leyla's anger at the dogs and their owner is, as one may suspect, white hot. As her Papa said in the aftermath, "If you have killer dogs, you have to have a killer fence."

Sadly, many of us saw the inevitability of this event just on the periphery and had discussed the dogs' aggression and the apparent need to reinforce the fence. Unfortunately for Sadie, and everyone who loved her cute eyes and tiny bark, we just did not understand how imminent the danger actually was. Sadie has been buried lovingly at Papa's, and Leyla and her family are trying to heal.

> Sometimes in the darkness there is a silver lining. We are all happy for this glimmer.

Little Miss Opal and Nana have been gone this past week in Sanibel Island- a beautiful place for quiet solitude and play. We are looking forward to Opal and Nana's return today, as well as the arrival of Leyla and Opal's Aunt Sue. Hopefully, this family time will be just what is needed to recover from a sad, bad week.

School starts on September 9th, and parents all over Ithaca are happily awaiting its return. I will give everyone an update on how all of the little ones do on their first day back. I plan to make the rounds, as all of our little girls get on the bus again to begin a new school year. Let's send love and a shout out to our teachers going back too; Katie, Rich, Enrique, and last but not least, my papa. We are wishing great things for our little and big people.

I will time my next update to coincide with Leyla's next MRI scheduled for September 5th. In the meantime, send Sadie some love in the afterlife and each other love in this life. It is clear, especially

change is...

in light of the events of this past week, that this is no dress rehearsal; but the real deal. As my Michael would say, "Go big or go home, little grasshopper." Make this life count my lovelies.

Big Love,

Jessica

big hearts and woven baskets

Dancing to Donna the Buffalo

Listening to Donna's sweet melodic voice was my sound track as I started falling. It still seems to be, because that was the first time Jared held me tight, as we spent our time dancing in the middle of a huge crowd. It was as if I had known him forever. Somehow it all seemed so familiar. Jared is one of the best things that has ever happened to me, though our relationship is very different from others. We share a deep love of life and are one another's solid ground. We share our sadness, our losses, and fears, but we too share our wishes and our dreams of our futures. There will never be a lack of love between us. I have never felt so loved in my entire life. As I go through this journey toward the unknown, he's right next to me. Summer rain falls over us, and we aren't complaining. A chilling rain and our warm hearts. The embrace of someone you love can make you feel infinite. I am alive. I am here, and I'm with you.

" *Love is, in fact, the best medicine.* "

Little People Big Hurts

It is a sweet day! Kiddos are back in school and all of the parents I know are super happy and relieved, and mostly not a bit sad to see them off this morning. Many of you are probably wondering how Leyla's MRI went last Thursday. It was a long and frustrating day for Leyla, Julia and Nana though, by all accounts, the tumor itself remains stable; no notable change, which is fantastic. Leyla will need to see a neurologist for the seizures she is having. Thus far, this does not seem to be urgent though it will be important to consider as we move forward.

Leyla has had a lovely last bit to her summer. She is, after all in LOVE! She has been spending lots of time with Jared, going to concerts and to barbecues and is also having slumber parties with her best girls, Melissa and Amy C. So all is blissful on that front.

One aspect of Leyla's life that has been very difficult for her is her relationship with Opal. Leyla is an amazing and loving sister, and Opal is a headstrong, do-it-herself kind of girl. We are all worried about Opal, who we know is hurting so much. Her life has been filled this past year with fear, uncertainty and emotions that her young self simply can't process. Opal is the kind of girl that you can love immensely and wholeheartedly, but she won't allow herself to be scared and vulnerable, even with those she loves most. She has built heavy, fortified walls around herself. Julia and Leyla are constantly trying to disassemble that wall, brick by brick, day in and day out.

Opal believes she is less loved, less important than Leyla. We know this is not true and that Opal is Leyla's single most adored loved one. While we cannot take away this pain for Opal, we can acknowledge that for her it is real. So, we ask you this… Send your love to Opal, and when you see her, let it shine brightly. Give her an extra hug and spend time letting her know just how very special she is. We give you our love and gratitude for your many kindnesses. You are bright, shiny and beautiful people.

Big Love,

Jessica

Courtesy of Jeffrey Foote Photography

Harvest Moon

We have had a beautiful full Harvest Moon this week. My hope is that you have all had a chance to bask in the pale moonlight. It is an extraordinary wonder, this natural world we live in. I would like to dedicate this update to another wonder, the wonder of family. A family's ecology is a bit like a fingerprint, no family is exactly alike. That being said, I would like to shine a light on Leyla's vast family; a web of beautiful translucent connections that rest on a strong foundation of love. Within this family is a safety net in which her whole world can take refuge and rest.

Earlier this week, Julia, struggling under the weight of the enormity of this journey, was able to rest in the comfort of her mother's love. Leyla had one of her slumber parties with her Katie and Rich and got to snuggle in with Stella and Augie in their quaint and perfect home. Opal spent a night at Nana's, and her Papa arrived early one morning to ferry her to school.

In tough times, family is sometimes the glue that holds us intact when we might otherwise shatter into a million pieces. In this family, when someone is having a bit of a difficult time, we will ask, "Do you need a mama?" Anyone needing a bit of extra love has a lot of mamas, be it an actual mama or a symbolic one.

. . . .

Family travels with you, wherever you are; you carry family in your soul and it fills your whole world.

. . . .

This is simply someone who will understand, nurture and love you till everything feels just a bit better. Mamas are just fine…and we love all of ours. Papas are also most welcome, and when we need an extra papa or two we just tell them to "mind their eggs," just like a good papa penguin would.

It is important to understand that family is not necessarily about blood connections, though that can be part of it. Family, in this village is a broader, more abstract concept with a tangible shared soul. This family is made up of loved ones, near and far who laugh with you, smile with you, and carry your grief for you when it is too heavy to carry alone.

When you have this kind of family, you understand that the best of the universe resides inside of you; because those you love share a space in the fabric of your being.

These times have been very tough as of late, and while Leyla, Julia, Opal and their family work through the challenges that this life bears, they do so with an abundance of being, an abundance of love, and unparalleled humility.

We are all connected in some way to one another. Look inside of you, find the glimmering web of connections that holds you together, honor those you love and you will find a family like Leyla's; only the fingerprint will be slightly different, though never less beautiful.

For me, I am going to take a peek and see who is shimmering deeply inside of my mind's eye on this dark night. Then, I am going to harvest all of my memories of those I love so very much, and snuggle them close to my heart.

Today, I am grateful for family, this vast web of people who I love to distraction and who make this life worth witnessing. Snuggle your peeps, take a glance inside and fortify. Spin your webs, and love without abandon; it makes for a great family.

Big Love,

Jessica

Bubble Tea and Pedicures

We have been busy little bees as of late, enjoying the early fall and our bright sun shiny days and cool clear nights. Leyla named last week "Opal's Never-Ending Birthday Week." There was a family celebration at Nana's, a family and friends BBQ, and an all-out dance party with disco lights and what felt like a million small people.

In keeping with our birthday theme, we celebrated more birthdays for our sisters Jasmin and Amy C., as well as for my lovely mother in the eternal realms. When you have this many birthdays, you must also witness the happy birthing days for all of the women that carried these beautiful humans in their bodies.

We enjoyed a beautiful Sunday, Leyla driving skillfully (with me riding shotgun and only slightly terrified) throughout Ithaca on her way to Nana's house for dinner. Once there, we sat on the back porch enjoying the sun and a light breeze. Nana was busy cooking individual miracles in the kitchen, and young loves lay in the lawn while Augie toddled here and there. A red tailed hawk flew above us and circled the fire trees of autumn, signaling good things to come.

There are big things on the horizon. The most freeing thing about Living Life Like Leyla is that the beauty of the universe is distilled, the beauty of family and friends is crystal clear; the wisdom of the Great Beyond peeks out from behind the veil that separates this world from all that exists beyond it. Therein lies unparalleled wonder. For now, we enjoy the simple things this life offers … bubble tea and pedicures. Cheers!

Big Love,

Jessica & Leyla

Move Over Billy Goats

I thought I would share with you that the sky fell in my dreams last night. My inner animators are working overtime, and I think they have the special effects pretty perfect. As is always the case with my dream life, I sit with these images and try to determine what tiny little gems lie inside.

I was with Julia earlier in the week during a moment of deep angst. I sat with her and we mused, and we walked, and mused some more. Through our conversation, the tangle of anxiety's grip lessened, as it so often does with mindful attention and reflection. Sometimes, we need to just cry deeply in our bodies, shiver with fear, and then find a tiny smile and true north. Julia, having felt this array of emotions, was able to re-orient herself once again, able to live inside her body instead of buzzing around the fringes with the terrible grating vibration of anxiety. After all, Julia has always been a glass half full person.

We all struggle each day in some way, some more than others, though in truth suffering is relative. We should all just shake our heads in dismay at the Gods on occasion—the cruel tricks they play. Sometimes we have to climb a mountain just to get out of bed to inhabit our bodies each day. But we get up anyway, and we lace our boots up just a little tighter, because today we have a mountain to climb. Bring a friend on your mountain journey, and don't forget to pack your gear. You don't have to be un-tethered. You can simply accept it and hug your mountain to your soul; wrap your arms tightly around it, securing yourself in your place.

Leyla has taught me that fully living means graceful acceptance that yes, in the end, we all die. In fact, we die a little each day; but before we ready ourselves for our backwards birthing, find the simple truth of the gift of this life. Let your life shine forth, be fully animated, fully alive. For those times when life feels so hard that you want to shed your skin and leave your body behind, "Live Life Like Leyla." Throw your clothes off and dive deep into the ocean, and call forth to her little mantra –"Just Keep Swimming!" Or if you are like my Amy, you will climb your mountain and feed a billy goat along the way, because mountains are for people too. While you hang out way up there on your beautiful mountain, reach down, pick up the sky and put it right back where it belongs.

Big Love,

Jessica

My Little Ones

To my sweet gentle Stella,

How I adore you. I am so lucky that I have gotten to create a bond with you ever since you were born. You read a few pages of a chapter book to me last night and it reminded me of how big you're getting. I am amazed at who you have become and I am so happy to call you my cousin. You tell me about your first grade life and I am happy to listen. You are a creative bird. I'm going to miss your laugh, and "Ley look, Ley look!" I love you, my Stel.

Oh little Augie,

You're growing so fast. Talking everywhere you go, yelling at everything you see. You see the tea kettle, "TEA, HOT!" with a very concerned look. You're putting things together and I'm still here to watch. I love watching you grow and learn. New life is beautiful and watching you has been such a gift to me that I still get to watch from this world. You are hysterical, you keep me laughing till my stomach aches. I love you bunches, and will watch you from the Great Beyond.

" Spread your light across this world. "

" You are a piece of my soul which travels beyond this life. "

blissful dying

Bamboo Is a Limited Diet

Sometimes you wake up and the whole world feels like it is sitting on top of you. As if a giant panda bear is sitting on your chest. While you stare in wonder of this beautiful life, you realize that you are slowly suffocating, and the terror of that knowledge is unbearable. Sometimes, all we can do is breathe slowly and with great deliberation until we realize that there is a light shining into the darkness that envelops us, and while that light is blinding it bears truth. Maybe in this truth we ultimately find comfort.

The fall is closing in on us and our village is strong and wide; we are fortifying for winter. Some things are primal and our instincts are on full alert. We are gathering spirit food for nurturing our souls. This past year has been incredibly humbling on so many levels. We readily accept the gift of this life, and we sit in love and heartache together as a single breathing organism.

Our Katie always says, "I am holding you in love and light," and that might just sum up the nucleus of Leyla's Village.

And when we wake up to this giant panda, who we love and revere so much sitting squarely upon our chests, we delight in its majestic beauty. And before this lovely creature squeezes the last breath from our bodies, the village turns itself inside out and breathes for us. And all of your mamas and sisters and daughters are not islands to take refuge in during the storm; we are the whole of the ocean. And all of these men we love, they harness the gravitational pull, making sure our ocean and all of her tides are just so.

Everyone needs to be held, everyone needs to be loved, and everyone needs light to shine on the darkest of moments. This is for all of you, the bright spirits of Leyla's Village. Live Katie's little mantra today, and hold someone in love and light. I am wrapping all of mine around Julia and Shana today. Our panda is hungry and needs some bamboo. Panda, you need to stop laying around on my girls' chests. Too heavy panda, too heavy…now come and eat.

Big Love,

Jessica

Are Impalas Vegetarians?

Leyla and I are tucked away in a perfect cabin retreat; we are snuggled in with our blankets and surrounded by a million pillows. We should mention that this is a hunting cabin, and we have company. After nervously eying the fox and only taking guarded glances at the impala, we decided we are here to stay and so are they. We have given both of these regal boys' names. Our little foxy fella is Margaret, and our impala with his beautiful eyes is Phoebe. We have decided we may invite them to join us for breakfast in the morning…We hope they like French toast, we are serving it with local maple syrup. We suspect Phoebe, being an impala, may be a vegetarian. Margaret gets her French toast with bacon.

We have alternately bundled ourselves on the couch, on the floor, and in blankets on the front porch watching the morning mist rise off the river. As we sit in the crisp air, drinking herbal tea, we rest in the moment and search our minds for hidden words and stories.

Our being together marks a simple joy and sparks our inner laughter. We talk long about living in the moment, how short life is, and how sad it is to waste it taking mundane things so seriously. We talk about the power of dreams, and how Leyla imagines herself moving to Montana with Jared on a big farm under an open, clear sky. She dreams of a houseful of children, and gardens, and laying in the grass soaking in the sky. We talk about the preciousness of time, and the gift of a singular moment. We talk of the foolishness of taking moments for granted, and how Leyla wants her life to remind people to fully inhabit each moment of their lives. To awaken to the inherent beauty of a moment in time, and to string them together with all of their shimmer, and trail them behind you, a twinkling reminder of where you have been.

Tonight we are deeply content, though I have been forbidden to play any more Loreena McKennitt this evening, as Leyla says that it is sucking the life out of her special moment and making her depressed around the edges. We opted for Van Morrison and more tea, which offered us lighter hearts and songbird voices, which are actually nothing like song birds. We fill our tummies with treats and our minds with one another, Leyla sharing with me that we have arrived in a different place together, one where we speak the same words from a single voice.

We are snuggling in soon, to wrap ourselves in heavy quilts and one another, bringing a close to our writing retreat, so we wrap up and talk long. Fear is creeping in on our girl, as she thinks about her chemotherapy that will end next week. We talk about the unknown and how it can have a grating harsh effect on our realities. While she is looking forward to the end of chemo side effects and marathon driving, she is feeling the weight of knowing that there will be no more medicine fighting the cancer that lives inside her body. So, let us collectively dive deep into the well-spring of hope and wrap ourselves in our love for Leyla, Julia, Opal and for one another. Sometimes love makes the whole world shine. Let's be luminous.

Big Love,

Jessica & Leyla

Be Here Now

Taking steps. I need a moment. I just want to slide to the floor for a minute. My family is my rock. They hold me up in the moments I feel shaky. They are my solid ground. My doctors were so glad last week when I ended chemo. I guess I was too and I am excited that I will get poked once every other week rather than twice. The little things, I am glad that I won't need toxic medicine infused into my body. The big things, I am allowed to be scared, though I am scared because there is now me, and the tumor and the cancer, and nothing to protect it. There isn't any more radiation to blast at my brain and no more chemo until further notice. Those are my fears.

Through all of this though, I've learned that your fears can be real, but enjoying what you've got will make a world of difference.

I am only 16 and I have everything I could ever want or need. I am lucky. This is the life I was given and there's nothing to do but love it. So I slide up from the floor, and I breathe.

I breathe for my life, I breathe for those who are now in the Great Beyond, who have fought this same fight. I am breathing for you. Taking steps. I am here, now.

❝ I have chosen my own path, and my path is not to dread the inevitable, but to live; truly live, with what I have. ❞

be here now

blissful dying

Courtesy of Jeffrey Foote Photography

Endless Happy Loop

This past week has been so full. Many of you know that Leyla's chemotherapy officially ended. Leading up to the appointment was an anticipation and anxiety that left us all desperate and starved for air. We were all able to breathe happily and with deep gratitude when we learned that Leyla's tumor remains stable. As you may imagine, this new phase of being treatment free is both liberating and terrifying. This cancer, this tumor still exists, and so does this life. We are hurdling through space and time toward the holidays, and this year the holidays will be uninterrupted by treatments. Our homes will be bursting at the seams with those we love next Thursday. We will wrap ourselves in this love and fill our souls with laughter; and then just for good measure we will repeat with a Saturday brunch. How we love an encore!

Another encore, though not of the food filled holiday kind, was a special event that Leyla attended on Saturday night as a guest (along with many friends) at the Blind Spots concert. To Leyla's happy surprise, Maddy and her band dedicated a song to her "Girls Just Want to Have Fun" a song they learned to play just for her.

And for a moment of extra juicy musical collaborative genius, Dan and Josh from the Gun Poets joined in to sing "Make you Happy," which just happens to be one of Leyla's all-time favorite songs. If you are not familiar with the Blind Spots or the Gun Poets, you most definitely need to check them out. They are brilliant musicians, and we love them for the joy they bring to our dancing gypsy souls. Also, they indulge our love of spending hours on end with a single song on repeat. Never underestimate a great song played a million times on an endless happy loop.

A mantra has been streaming through my world this past week, something Shana wrote on the last day of Leyla's treatment. "Grateful for so much today. Grateful it is possible... count your blessings and your challenges. In the end, you owe them both your wisdom." This life is so complex; our paths are ever twisting in time and our hearts float on the changing currents of wind through sky. Live in your joy and gratitude whenever possible, and when your path becomes rocky, meet yourself where you are at and trod on. There is always a special unknown right around the bend.

Big Love,

Jessica

Courtesy of Dave Burbank Photography

Utterly Breathless

We have just floated past the Thanksgiving holiday on an endless ribbon of shiny gratitude. We had many a gathering, sleepover, and some truly amazing shared meals together. There can be no price placed on spending time in the company of those you love best. We spent the holiday in just the places that we needed to be, basking in the glow of those we love.

Our dark afternoons have prompted us to take extra care, nap a bit, have a midnight chat, and rest covered in warm blankets on the couch like happy hibernating bear children. We hope your holiday was filled with exactly what you needed, that the cauldron of your heart was bubbling with the joy of family, friends and gratitude.

We are incredibly grateful that our time together still beats on. We are looking towards the winter solstice with knowledge that we are full of new adventures and new beginnings. We look forward to the increased light that will shine with us as we make our way into Christmas and the celebration of a New Year. We have so much to celebrate! We hope you will join us for the biggest celebration Ithaca is likely to see this holiday season. We hope to see your shiny faces at the Haunt this Sunday. I imagine it will be unlike anything we have ever known. Perhaps our abundant, joy, laughter, gratitude, humility, peace and kindness will burst out of the building, glide across the waters of Cayuga Lake and onto the wind currents of space and time.

Leyla's Village has been blessed over and over again. We have been gifted with time, the most complex and utterly simple equation of all. Time is most central in my mind's eye in this moment, for without it, all of this beauty would not be growing in the gardens of our lives. Maya Angelou said, "Life is not measured by the number of breaths we take, but by the moments that take our breath away." Leyla shares this truth with us each day. We are utterly breathless.

Big Love,

Jessica

> We are undeterred by darkness, as nothing can prevent us from creating our own light.

Dancing on Frozen Nights

My heart is achingly full and bursting with sheer gratitude to each one of you for all the love you all brought to the Haunt last night. Leyla's Village is not only a lovely reflection of what she brings to this extraordinary life, but an amazing and crystal clear reflection of each of you and our beautiful community.

I am completely undone by your boundless unrestrained love, your generosity of spirit, and the shiny and blissful joy that you bring to Leyla and her family each day. I wish in my life that I could see auras, though in reality this divining is not needed for any one of you. It is ever apparent that your souls shimmer with a kind, gentle and rare beauty.

We are quickly approaching the darkest day of winter, a time when many choose to stay in, summoning their inner bear, intent on a deep hibernation only to truly emerge when the sun greets us again and the unlocking of spring is released with the melting ice and growing things. I loved that so many of you shed your bear skins to join Leyla and her family last night. On my drive home afterward, I imagined that the moon was desperate to leave the sky to dance with wild abandon with each of you to the music we were blessed with.

What you bring to Leyla's Village shines into the rest of the world. Every day, your many kindnesses, your love and your deep compassion make the world a better place. Your souls flutter like the wings of a butterfly touching places and people you may never go or meet, your beauty in this world is unparalleled.

It is dark and early my friends. I am going to climb into my skin for a winter nap. If you choose to do the same, dream of your goodness and know how very special you are to Leyla and to us who love her so.

Big Love,

Jessica

blissful dying

Sky Mind

> *My head is facing the sky. I need a second, just a moment to breathe and hold myself. Oh, this is a wide, wide world. I am a grateful girl.*

Take Out Thai

Gearing up to Christmas was an interesting exercise in endurance and organization (or disorganization as the case may be), fueled by takeout Thai food and frozen yogurt. We crazily wrapped gifts and stowed them under the tree, and sported oddly achy backs for our trouble.

We laughed lots, and if truth be known, we complained a bit as well. Leyla was very busy orchestrating Opal's gift—a completely re-designed bedroom. Leyla and Papa painted it a fresh sea foam blue with colorful lanterns hung from the ceiling.

Courtesy of Jeffrey Foote Photography

Together, they included all of the glittery, sparkling touches that Opal so loves. Nana and Opal were busy crafting many projects, and Leyla went off with Katie and Rich to bake Christmas cookies with Kathleen. The holiday overall was a bit different, in some ways difficult and in others quite filled with beauty and gratitude. Santa has now come and gone and Julia and family are getting on with the business of greeting a new year.

Leyla has been experiencing some unusual symptoms and at times has been feeling pretty rotten. Because of this, her MRI originally scheduled for late January will take place tomorrow in the late afternoon in Rochester. Jared will go with Leyla, making this trip a bit brighter for her.

We will let you know as soon as results are in, though it is unlikely to be before Thursday. We all hope to greet the New Year tomorrow with light hearts, so after their return, Julia, Leyla and Opal will gather with friends at home to usher in the New Year.

For now, let's contemplate some of our bright spots in 2013, in no particular order. Gingerbread man birthday candles, a wide beach full of laughing girls and umbrellas to shade Augie from the bright sunshine, pickle ball, shouting with joy as Leyla saw her VW convertible bug for the first time, harvest moons, lazy afternoons with our feet dangling in Opal's kiddie pool, Northstar, Shana's unexpected arrival for Leyla's birthday, falling in love, Ali announcing that she is expecting a baby boy, holding beautiful Sadie while she snuggled on the couch, polar bear swims in Cayuga Lake, slumber party dance-a-thon with all of our big and little girls, watching Kathleen rub sand into her skin all while smiling at the ocean, a weekend in Vermont, driving with the top down, slumber parties with Margaret the fox and Phoebe the impala, dancing the days and nights away at Grassroots, ping pong, the gift of watching our sleeping children, being the boss of ourselves, bonfires, slow cooked ribs and macaroni and cheese, leaning back on Nana's deck watching hawks circle the brightly colored fall trees, Betty Boop costumes and the wondrous Uni-Clown, being dazzled by the Blind Spots, the Gun Poets, Sim Redmond Band, and Bronwen Exter, "human xanax", couches filled with slumbering girls, Leyla's photo shoots, cruising the lake on the Cacciotti's boat, notes of love from Leyla's Village and last, but certainly not least: time.

• •

Be light of heart tomorrow, be whimsical, let your souls dance on the cold winter winds.

• •

We wish you an amazing journey in 2014, one filled with family, friends, abiding happiness, bright detours, and the unparalleled beauty of just being alive.

Big Love,

Jessica

take out thai

Beats

Yesterday, I laid in the MRI machine, closing my eyes, just knowing. I made lyrics to the sound of the banging, slamming, and beeps. Breathing and knowing, and being okay with it.

My tumor has begun to grow again. I am feeling so many different things. My initial reaction was and is, just overwhelmed and confused. But then, I simply realized that since my diagnosis I have found myself and the meaning of my life; that it is not the time spent on this earth, but the way you live it. I chose to live happily. I woke up today, to my mom, my sister, my family, to Jared and that means the world to me. My oncologist will be meeting with several doctors to figure out the next step. Please hold those I love in your hearts today. And don't forget to smile today; after all, you woke up, and you are alive.

> **" *I can easily say,*
> *my life is amazing.* "**

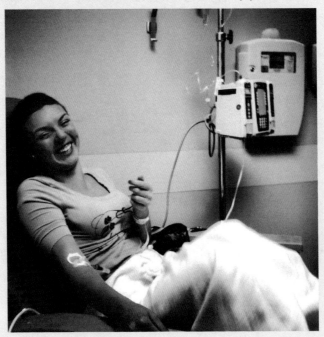

The Bones of Wisdom

It has been a bit of time since we last checked in, though many of you know that the results of Leyla's latest brain scan came back last Thursday. For those of you who don't know, Leyla's tumor has begun to grow again. The growth is fairly significant from the previous one taken at the end of November. These are soul shattering moments, and Papa rocked Leyla gently on his lap as he has so many times before, and held her as she cried, silently putting the pieces of her back together. For while we are all struggling to wrap our minds around this turn of events, we are not surprised.

The knowing of this trajectory was in our bones, and still we hoped that the reprieve would be longer. Leyla and Julia met with Dr. Korones today. They have shared with Leyla her options and included the timeframe that she can expect to remain with us. Leyla has the option of resuming a rigid course of treatment or abstaining from treatment and living out her natural life course. Leyla and Julia are doing as best as they can with this heavy news, and are enjoying, as much as possible, a mother-daughter day of shopping and dinner out.

In the coming days, Leyla will have the opportunity to explore her own life path, and with loving support will choose what is best for her. Once Leyla decides for herself how she will spend her remaining days, her family and her abundant circle of friends will hop on board and join her for the ride. We are so immensely grateful for the last year and look forward to ushering this New Year forth. There is much to savor in this life: cold snaps and gymnastics, tropical travel and hot tea, snapshots of Leyla and Jared under a random and gigantic painting of a boy cow, the sound of Augie calling out, "Jukes! Jukes!" and unraveling the mysteries of archaic meets new generation technology.

So, under this waxing gibbous moon and the quiet night sky we sit in the here and now. We accept the inescapable truth that the sands of time for each of us slip away, grain by grain and moment by moment. And while time shortens for us all, if we are lucky, the moments we fully experience life grow wildly, sending our roots deep into the earth, and all the while growing beautiful flowers that reach for the sun and the sky. We are simply going to lie down in the grass and enjoy her landscape and hopefully plant a flower or two of our own. There is much growing to do—sink your roots in deep and reach for the sun.

Big Love,

Jessica

> Leyla is a master of capturing the moment, and in savoring the beauty of it; her soul garden is wild, untamed, and bright.

To Our Twin Souls

Your momma said yesterday that God must have understood that a single child would never have been enough to fill the void Leyla will leave in our lives; so the Gods in their infinite wisdom blessed her with two shimmering, soul children.

It was a cold day when we learned of your presence. We were having dinner with your Momma (Julia), Leyla, Opal, Papa, and Michael. We stood in the kitchen and glanced at the sonogram. It took only moments to realize that we were being blessed with more than one of you, and the two of you simply overwhelmed us with joy. We danced about and shouted, Amy and I somehow feeling that we had magically influenced the universe to bring in another pair of twins for our family.

Papa brought your mother flowers. He included goldenrod in the handpicked bouquet along with a note scribbled on scrap paper full of happy words. Opal was unable to contain her excitement, and leapt from one couch cushion to the next, somersaulting and full of smiles.

We mused about creating a suite downstairs for Leyla and talked animatedly about when you would be born and how enormous your momma would be carrying the two of you inside her body.

Weeks later, our excitement is still bursting at the seams. We chatter about you daily, argue about what you will be named and whether you are boys or girls, and if you will be soft spoken or have loud voices that make us want to wear noise canceling headphones. We are anxious, anxious, anxious for your arrival and just love you to pieces already.

Big Love,

Jessica & Amy

I Define Me

Cancer Awareness Day. Hold those you love in your hearts.
Cancer does not define me. I am sick, I am happy, and I am full of life.
Cancer does not define me, because I know who I really am and
cancer isn't it.
Cancer doesn't define me because I
was born into a beautiful, loving,
warm family.
Cancer does not define me because
I choose to live in the utter truth of
my death, and still I stand in the
sunshine.
Cancer does not define me because I
stand in the pouring rain in silence
and smile because I am here.
Cancer doesn't define me because
this is inevitable and it does
not overcome my love of life.
Inevitable, blissful, dying.
Cancer does not define me because
I see the bliss in waking up,
making tea, being in the deepest
love with Jared, walking on the
pavement, seeing my sister smile,
seeing my beautiful mother and the man she loves bring
something so joyful to our lives. Our twins, I'm fighting to meet you.
Cancer does not define me because no matter what happens, I have lived
such a beautiful life. And cancer cannot take that away from me.

Family Under Construction

So many exciting things have happened since we last checked in! Fasten your seatbelts, we are going to take you on a ride! In recent news, our Leyla is three treatments into her new course of chemotherapy, a full six weeks and counting. The first treatment was unbearably harsh, and she spent many hours and days lying in her mom's arms. All this terrible while, Julia just held her close, made her tea, and brought her bits of food. Thankfully, the subsequent treatments have been getting a bit easier...Despite these treatments, Leyla dazzles us with her humor. She has officially decided to haunt some people in her afterlife, and she insists that her funeral have bouncers to keep out undesirables; I am happy to announce none of you are on this list. She also made her mom promise that she would not be a creepy mama and keep her room untouched

like a mausoleum in her grief, and also that she cannot empty her room the day she dies. We love that humor is still abundant, and though at times it is dark, it instantly creates lightness in us all.

In other family news...Julia, Leyla and Opal's family has doubled. Well, more than doubled if we count the slumbering twins. Jamon, Julia's boyfriend and his children Tahjay and Aysia have been happily welcomed into the family.

You will learn much about them in the coming weeks, months and years, but this is their official debut. Jamon has his hands full with Julia and her "pregnancy brain." She needs a personal manager. Just for the record, he also rocked out a Valentine's Day card that told Julia the secret of his love for her; that he loves her more than bacon, and he really loves bacon. Don't we all?

Tahjay turned 15 on Valentine's Day, and Julia made a big family dinner. They celebrated along with the whole and ever growing clan. Tahjay also moved in her two leopard geckos (Bonnie and Clyde) so they must also be counted as family. Taj likes to act and will be in an upcoming school play. She is a lovely character. Aysia wanted you all to know that she is 87, going on 10. She wants, wants, wants an iPhone for her upcoming birthday (which she will not get), wields a nasty light saber, and plays basketball on her school team. We just love these kids and this growing family! Opal rushed in this evening, a bundle of excited energy and smiles. She is still the loudest child we all know, and has just increased her volume as there are now more voices to conquer. She reminded me that she is a keeper of secrets, though I can't vouch for her as a secret keeper as she won't even tell me what secrets she is privy to. Papa is up to his old antics, and will be crashing the upcoming Sanibel Island vacation where he will join Leyla, Jared, Opal and Nana. Papa is busy warning his loved ones about the dangers of soda and praising the merits of pickle ball.

Nana is recently returned from Guatemala and quickly arranged the Sanibel Island trip. Nana is a doer, she is like the mother of Superwomen everywhere. She is busy cooking Sunday dinners and generally being amazing.

In other family news… Spencer has Julia's house under construction. He is banging around and sawing things and creating just the right amount of chaos. After all, we must build space for this growing clan. Leyla and Jared just celebrated their six month anniversary at ZaZa's, and are mostly inseparable and so cute we can't stand it.
Finally, we are totally excited, and perhaps a bit crazy with the waiting for these upcoming babies.

Ali and Paul will shine us into spring with their baby boy and Julia and Jamon will welcome their babies in the first days of summer. Augie, now the biggest of the tinies, will be heading up the motorcycle club that they will all join 18 years from now.

Sometimes life shines bright in the darkest moments. Our clever universe hunts us down to smile upon us, even when we are huddled on the kitchen floor sneaking a quick cry. The past, present and future are ever converging, making this life journey endless and amazing. Our hearts are full of miracles big and small.

Big Love,

Jessica

family under construction

Through the Leaves of Trees

I was born into a family that I have simply adored from the beginning. Life looks like the big tree at Papa's that my momma used to set me under. I was amazed at the leaves and the wind. Learning the first bits of life. Life is like the comfort of my sweet momma holding me tight. Life is like sitting on the porch swing with Papa after a summer's day.

Life is like the sweet voice of my Katie singing me to sleep. Life is like Opal, my golden curly haired sister who is full of life and seems to have a deep knowing beyond this world. Life is like my uncle Rich who piles tons of wool blankets on me when I'm asleep to just make sure I'm warm. Life is like my sweet Stella, who I can't help but adore, practicing her songs with such confidence, a baby who would just sit and draw, and think to her quiet little self. Augie, our boy! Reciting "In the Night Kitchen" quotes at one and a half, with that raspy voice and huge smile.

*" **Life is like sitting on the porch swing with Papa after a summer's day.** "*

Life is like Jamon's laugh and hand on my momma's belly. Life is like Aysia. American Idol judges we are, her laugh is contagious. Life is like Tahjay, busting dance moves while she holds lizards on her shoulder. Life is like these babies that will soon enter into this beautiful world; we are patiently waiting for you.

Life is like Ali; her love for Pauly, her bubbly personality and baby bump full of a gift to the world. Life is like Shana, who keeps me hysterically laughing and always knows the right thing to say. Life is like Kathleen and Rick with their warmth and unconditional love.

Life is like Jared, dancing under the moon, full of light, warmth, and a love like no other. He has a laughter that comes from deep inside. Life sounds like laughter, and when it all comes together, it is so special. It is life. It is love.

Sending Love,

Leyla

The Gypsy Daughter of Chemo

The past month has been a happy, albeit slushy and at times frigid, sleet filled April. We are chilly and starved for sunshine, so when the sun shines bright we are hungrily seeking light and air, growing towards the sun like a crocus in blossom. Leyla returned from her vacation with Nana in Mexico, an almond brown beauty. She is as fresh and relaxed as an afternoon, sun kissed nap. Leyla is responding well to chemotherapy and her physicians have integrated a new post chemo therapy regimen of medications to help her keep the body-wrenching side effects at bay. This past chemo treatment, Leyla was joined by Jared, Opal and Aysia along with the esteemed Momma Julia.

The girls danced like banshee wild children, happy and light while Leyla's chemotherapy dripped, dripped, dripped, through her veins. Happy, bliss-filled children's innocence makes our world's cares obsolete. Life is truly well and good. Our children, big and small, and babies in waiting are the mark of our daily miracles. We breathe them all in and absorb their wonderment and are grateful for these many blessings we are a part of and witness to.

Nana, Katie and Rich have made a major transition, though all of it occurred in a few miles radius. Our families traded houses! Katie, Rich, Stella and Augie have taken over Nana's sprawling house with giant property and outbuildings alike, while Nana moved into Katie and Rich's wonderful, quaint pink home. This is a most welcome transition. Creating space for a growing family where expansiveness and exploration is deeply desired and inviting a close and intimate space for our Nana who needs less and less space to find her joy.

Leyla and I have been so excited this week to host a small gathering of family and friends to unveil a surprise long in the making. We dreamed of our loved ones' joyful, surprised faces and were so delighted that so many of our sweet clan showed up for our celebration. Melynda booked our venue in our favorite tapas bar overlooking the lake and the blooming trees of spring. Michael, who actually showed up on time carried in boxes full of books and stowed them hidden under tablecloths, and the rest of us ordered drinks. Once settled in, Leyla invited her family to unveil her gift of Blissful Dying to each of them. It was a delicious day, full of stolen moments to read a page or two, laughter, and friends, and last, but definitely not least, pregnant designated drivers.

We are fully on baby watch now, with Miss Ali on deck with Paul and the incoming sweet Waylon, Katie and Josh with their baby boy and Julia and Jamon with their twin girls bringing up the rear. We have few boundaries when it comes to their pregnancies, sometimes greeting their swollen bellies with kisses and a whisper to babies before we even greet their mothers. We can often be seen feeling for a baby foot, or massaging terribly rude and swollen feet and legs, that have come to resemble tree trunks.

We wish you a fertile spring, one full of growth and rejuvenation. Lift your faces to the sunshine friends, and bask in the joy of light. Our hearts are open and lifted, to ourselves, to one another, and to you. May your coming days be full of radiance and your glowing hearts be full of love, hope and rebirth.

Big Love,

Jessica

Wondermama

This Mother's Day we find that we wish to spread our love for our mothers' spinning through time; a backwards reflection of delightful persuasion. We are mindful and present to our gift of being born into this world by mothers whose strong, fierce, and kind love flowed forth freely; growing our young selves into the women we have become.

Leyla loves to float in our sea of mamas, and Mother's Day is no exception. We have raised her to know that the inherent love of our sisterhood provides us with the perfect ingredients to raise up a batch of babies ever so sweet. We are mamas who learned from our own to create wonder from seemingly nothing, and who created and play the Glad game with astounding frequency. We have learned that the faces of motherhood are ever changing, because we are ever growing. This means our children are likely to need therapy, because well…we are human and so are they.

Mothers are an intricate tapestry of archetypical genius. We are crescent moon bear mamas, strong, self-sufficient, instinctual and deeply protective. We are Persephone, birthing children from flowers on our heads. We are trickster, and cheerleader, and milk machine. We are mean aunt so- and so- at bedtime, and we touch the multitude of ever moving arms of our sweet Goddess Devi. She inspires us to move in ways that result in simultaneously packing lunches our kids will actually eat, while talking on the phone, drinking coffee and flagging down a school bus.

> Can I point out that my mom is an amazing woman? You are a superhero. We got this!

We know that motherhood is a delicious, delightful, and at times a deeply painful gift, for when our children stir inside of us we just know that they will carry our love out of our bodies at birth and into the uncertain world. Knowing this truth makes us laugh a lot, and worry our pulses pretty much all of the time. This beautiful and painful gift allows us to understand that love is so exquisite because it is so perfectly fragile.

So our beloved tribe: snuggle your kiddos tight, and let your laughter light up your mother love.

So, for all of our mothers who make the get up and go look like a walk in a field of sun flowers we are loving you big each and every day. Leyla has always been the first of our children to spring out of bed in the morning to love her mama up big. Mother's Day and every day is a most excellent moment in time to honor yo mamas' array of mad skills.

Big love,

Jessica & Leyla

blissful dying

Twins

To my two sweet siblings who will soon arrive, you have filled my heart with a joy that I never knew was possible. You are coming into this world, while I slowly get closer to the Great Beyond; I am sending you all the love that I won't be able to show while you grow. Not seeing someone physically does not mean their soul is not present.

Dear babies, you are encrypted in my soul. You are permanently a part of me. Your life is a gift. You are my miracles. Welcome to this beautiful world.

I love you, I love you.

Leyla

> **" Life is a journey, and I am so happy I had you as part of mine. "**

The Land of Pond Porch

We have finally stumbled upon spring! It is the unlocking time, and our trees and grass are turning green and we have colorful flowers to mark our season. Ali and Paul's little boy is growing each day and truly has shined us into the spring season. He has already had a ride with his daddy on the tractor. We are just full of loving happiness for his tiny self, his long divine fingers and alert, curious gaze.

We have all taken full advantage of the blessed sunshine, last weekend meeting for a barbeque at The Land, our family nature oasis. Aysia, Opal, Emma and Sophie hiking, digging for worms, writing down their nature observations and collecting unsuspecting and alarmed toads. They screamed happily as they leapt off the pond porch, to swim and splash around in the pond. At one point the kiddos, mothers and dogs were all in the pond, at which time we watched as a wonderfully round bikini clad pregnant Julia sprang off the dock with me yelling, "hold those babies in!" I marveled at the perfect design of the human body, so shock absorbent. I am not even sure the twins woke from their quiet slumber upon hitting the water. Leyla and I pushed Julia's butt up the ladder, which in reality she had no trouble climbing; we just wanted to be helpful. Tahjay and Jamon played "brain-teasers'" I mean games on their phones and we marveled at Tahjay's expansive vocabulary (not the naughty kind, the lofty spelling bee kind). Jamon and Eli rode their motorcycles in and the rest of us drove cars full of children, dogs, coolers. The Gods are truly the silent architects of third row seating and hatchbacks. We did not have to leave anyone behind, and we still had room for fishing gear and tackle boxes. Tahjay, Jamon, and Enrique all caught fish; I hate to say it was a competition, but Tahjay totally won. I must add that Sophie was not fishing as she would have given them a run for their money.

Send lots of hope, healing and love today to Leyla as she begins a new round of daily radiation for the next several weeks. Her tumor, "Anjelica," is not playing nice and is growing fat, with a very thick skin and no regard for her host. She had a baby tumor without even soliciting an invitation! I mean REALLY…! This child tumor has yet to be named, but was measured carefully and duly noted by our medical marvels and basically getting all of the attention of an unwanted guest. Not to be deterred from fun or red meat, the whole family celebrated the beginnings of a new radiation journey by going to Outback Steakhouse-any excuse for a steak I suppose. Let us send Leyla a universal love push as she resumes life with an abundance of shiny beams of light.

There is much excitement in the wings, and Leyla will soon be attending the Mountain Jam music festival along with Papa and Rich, as a guest of Michael Franti. She will get to meet with Michael directly through his foundation, Do It For The Love. Following on the heels of this will be our anxious awaiting of the birth of the twins, her one year anniversary with Jared, Grassroots Music Festival and family vacation on Bethany Beach at the end of the summer. Phew!

Oh, the fun that awaits! Leyla continues to fill our lives with joy and grace, her presence has unlocked the doors to the sky-minds in us all; from this great place of awakening we can bear witness to her simultaneously shining our own joy and grace into the world. Touch your own love and grace, and witness it in yourselves and give it freely to others. We are love wealthy, and full of gratitude.

Big Love,

Jessica

the land of pond porch

XOXO to My Girls

Meli,

Whether we were 8 years old having modeling shows down the catwalk of our self-made living room runway, or sending good vibes to people while blasting reggae, there has never been a shortage of laughter between us. Cracking up about how funny we are, and wondering why we aren't already comedians. I mean...we. are. hilarious. Living right down the street from one another, we have been together basically every day... Taking pictures in the street, blasting music with Kat, ghost hunting with Brenda and singing to the gardeners. Going to California and Myrtle Beach. You are a friend I can always look at and know suddenly what you are thinking, the same way you can with me. You are truly my other half.

" My life wouldn't be the same without you. "

Amy,

I am simply thanking you for being an incredible friend. Over all of these years so much has changed. From the time we got to go Trick or Treating without adults, to getting my VW bug, to my diagnosis, you have been around for it all. Our nights at the beach, planning to get up for sunrise only to snooze our alarms 20 times. In 7th grade diving into the baby jellyfish that looked like Rice Krispies, even creepier when we accidentally maybe swallowed them. Thank you for these moments. Sometimes you only listened, and sometimes that is all I needed. Thank you for being here through it all. My soul will linger still. Don't give up, this life is a scary, beautiful ride. But trust me, it's worth the adventure.

" I love you, A. "

America's Next Top Model

Michael MC, aka Mr. Drama,

You would coach Kat, Meli and me, TV remote in hand presenting us to the invisible crowd for America's Next Top Model. You always did have a thing for Brats dolls, and cat walks. You taught me to play my first video game, and left me by myself to ride an elephant alone during our trip to the African Lion Safari, in Canada. Don't worry, I got even with you many times by painting your fingernails, and now I am getting back at you with this crazy picture.

Kat,

My little big sister, I still love how you danced around the dinner table and how everyone would join along. You were the bees' knees of sister-hood.

Meli,

This is a photo for you, a throwback to our modeling days.

Summer Is a Sprint Marathon

We have flown through our sunny spring and have finally encountered the warm weather we love so much. Motorcycles are tuned up, picnic baskets have been unearthed and our sweet children are handpicking flowers to delight their parents. The last month has greeted us with an astounding blur of joy, blessings, events, and reflections.

Here goes the random and colorful conglomeration of wonderfulness. Kiddos are out of school! Woo hoo!; and just few paces behind them followed Katie, Enrique and my papa. There were a smash of birthdays in June which we happily celebrated, on many occasions separately, and at least on one occasion together. Nana led the birthday pack, Amy and I sandwiched in the middle, with Katie only hours behind. There were 108 sun salutations (and sore arms), and cakes, and flowers, and sunbathing, and pond frolicking. Lots of chatter, kids on blankets, dogs on blankets, musical chair like carpooling, deliciously contrived foods and at least one duplicate salad of stolen nature.

There were concerts to be taken in, and celebrities to meet. Leyla, Jessica (not this one), Papa and Rich took in Mountain Jam Festival as a special guest of Michael Franti, and Do It For The Love Foundation. They listened to music through the sun-kissed day, and late into the night, catching the Allman Brothers, and narrowly escaping a storm. Rich took Katie to see Willie Nelson, which I hear was amazing.

In other news, Leyla is fully licensed and insured and she is all sapphire convertible, top down driving crazy. Often, she has many mothers shouting after her all at once, "Leyla drive safe, Leyla wear your seatbelt, Leyla don't turn the music up too loud;" to which she smiles her promise and leaves us all staring after her. And in her beautiful absence we all just shake our heads in wonderment, our sweet bird is free.

So much to share, so little time…here goes the sprint to the finish. Leyla has only three more sessions of radiation, and she is being shepherded there by all the women who love her and the men she can never leave behind. Jared has jumped the pond for a spin around France and Ireland before circling back to her. Julia is packed for twin arrival, and teetering on

Barney Rubble feet. Oh you girls, so naughty playing these tricks on your mama—you are so much like Leyla and Opal already with wanting to make your mother's legs root like trees. We are eager to evict these beauties from the womb, and gather them up in loving arms. There are excited sisters, brothers, aunties, uncles, cousins, a Nana, a Nāna, a Papa and a patiently, adoring father.

Onward, to Grassroots, and tan lines, fireflies, and baby cries and, of course, a well-timed "girls' hour out," Leyla baby—you are with us... the rest of our littles, we will leave you to the loving care of your Nanas and Papas.

Put on your running shoes and join us, we are just getting started. We have many miles to cover and a universe overflowing with bliss to chase. Turn your face to the sunshine, and play in the rainstorm, dangle your feet in the water and touch your gratitude; every single delicious moment is yours.

Big Love,

Jessica

Courtesy of Jeffrey Foote Photography

summer is a sprint marathon

Oh, Babies, Babies, Babies, Leyla's Village!

As many of you may know, Julia and Jamon welcomed their twins Violet and Esmae into the world late last night. Evidently, we can come to the conclusion that they were both comfortable in Julia's womb, and a bit stubborn in vacating their home. Julia was induced yesterday morning and labored throughout the day with Jamon and Leyla, Nanas and Aunties. Leyla provided a frenzied group of us with regular updates that sent us spinning with excitement and anticipation. We were slightly crazed, back seat driver, benched-player; wanna-be onlookers simply starved for news. Nana held down the family fort on Hancock St., washed windows, tended children and generally nested in her anticipation.

And then, the moment arrived! Well, not really…Shana, in her ever so awesomeness, announced the twins' arrival well before their actual appearance. Of course, this sent many of us (me included) into a celebratory whirl of shouting, toasting, dog barking, Face Time joy, and then ultimately into slight disbelief and confusion, which will certainly be told year after year when we tell the girls the story of their birth. Shana went radio-silent after turning my water into wine as she had a previous engagement with Vanilla Ice.

As we celebrated, and then sought clarification, Julia was entering the final stages of labor and surely wished that she had given birth to these girls already. Julia and Jamon spent the last of their laboring together in the operating room, where Violet came out head first and Esmae, well not so much. This was anticipated, and her obstetrician, an ever so talented fisherman was able to easily hook Miss Esmae by the feet and reel her into the world.

Violet and Esmae are beautiful and healthy, as is our favorite mama, Julia. Jamon also made it through the birthing process and did not even require an epidural in his efforts. Once the twins were born, Leyla sent the all-clear to immediate family who were so excited to meet the girls and then spent time welcoming her sisters to their first few minutes in this world. Opal, Aysia and Tahjay, snuggled the babies as well and had some wonderful bonding time with their parents and one another. Jamon keeps calling his beautiful Esmae, "black Jukes," and while the resemblance is spot on, we will try and find a nickname that is a bit snappier and as pretty as she is. Violet is

blissful dying

fair and looks remarkably like Jamon… Again, "white Jamon" is not a nickname we will allow to stick. Both girls are hungry little caterpillars, and nursed without delay as soon as they found their way into Julia's arms. Jamon will stay buff as he perfects the baby hand-off/ switch routine which will surely occupy much of his time. For now, we are overwhelmed with blessings and the whole-ness of us all. We are utterly grateful for Jared's happy homecoming, and his pond crossing adventures, and for the safe return of Melynda and Enrique from Peru.

    There is an endless stream of goodness to share. We are so proud of Jamon, as this week he undertakes a new career as a fire fighter with the City of Ithaca. It should be mentioned that he will also be the first black man to join this elite firefighting team. So, go Jamon! and also, come back Jamon!…(he will be leaving for fire academy soon). Leaving his kiddos, including new twins as well as his Julia, will be a hard sacrifice in these early days, though as a family it will be incredible in the long term. Shana promises a visit to take over Jamon's task of baby rocking, nursing delivery person, and general one-stop do it all human in his absence. For the record, she is also likely to do a lot of baby dressing up and picture taking.

    My Amy has already been to the hospital, and is busy breaking hospital rules against placing babies together in the bassinet. It is sometimes hard to understand twin speak and twin logic, though you all will become very accustomed to it in the coming days and years. Amy, with her abundant wisdom of all things twins, made sure before she left that the girls were snuggled together. She would have preferred that they be snuggled together and naked but Julia put her foot down, saying no-way…too cold in the hospital for this womb-making reenactment.

    Julia and Jamon are basking in love and kindness for their wonderful and BIG family. We are astonishingly in love, and living fully in the moment of our mid-summer's dream. Over and Out.

Big Love,

Jessica

There were happily shed tears and bed times long surpassed, as the whole clan joined the rest of the family at the hospital to greet our new wonders.

oh, babies, babies, babies, leyla's village!

Memories of Gypsy Feet

To my warm Nana, who I can still cuddle up to like a child. What would my world be without you Nana? Your love is magical and full of the most precious of mysteries. I was given a special gift from you, these traveling gypsy feet. These feet will carry me into the Great Beyond. I will carry your magical love with me deep into this world of the unknown. I love you my sweet Nana.

These gypsy feet of mine, have happily floated above the water on Nonni and Nonno's boat. Leaping from this boat with my family and swimming in the cold lake waters, this laughter still bubbles inside of me, making my soul shine. Dancing in your living room to the Grateful Dead, you help me to free my spirit. Life is beautiful and bright when I am with you.

Linda, you taught my little child's mind the love of art and wonder. Farmer's Market on a late summer's day, I could sit in my bliss in Marley's great openness. You see the world Marley, with tender and joyful eyes. To my laughing soul garden mamas. Shana, you light my world on fire. I am your bunny-child, and you are my den mama. Jasmin, our endless girl talks over *arroz con gandules* cooking lessons; you are my home away from home. My tiny girl feet have grown big in your presence. Amy, (mine) you are a brave and thoughtful force, my Gandhi mama full of life wisdom. You raced me to a faux hawk, just to show me the path forward; and for the record you won.

Loving you,

Leyla

memories of gypsy feet

Little Bees Full of Summer

Happy evening sweet Leyla's Village, we hope you are enjoying the last bit of summer. It is a perfect evening for eating an ice cream cone (with sprinkles of course), and generally making excellent plans for the last days before school starts. Leyla recently went to Taughannock Park and jumped right in the water; she said it made her feel very alive! It is, after all, our beautiful and rather frigid lake, and as for hopping in—well, it is summer's rite of passage.

Leyla and Jared celebrated their anniversary and most likely ordered Thai. That memory is a bit like a summer haze, but the ring he gave her—not hazy at all! It is so beautiful, and Leyla loves it so very much

Leyla has an MRI this Thursday and we are all hopeful that the results will be in the same day. Leyla uses a cane at times to help her get around more easily and her doctors have added a daily steroid. Orient your heart her way and send her your wide, limitless love.

The rest of the crowd has been busy, a hive of happenings; it is no wonder that Jamon recently added a tattoo of all his little bees. This is a most literal occurrence, no metaphor needed for his little winged, and buzzing wonders; all overseen by his queen bee. As Jukes would say, "totes approps." Well

played Jamon, well played. He is in week four of fire academy, and is missing all of his babies. He is still challenged by the sheer demand of the academy, what with all of the 5 AM crazy-must be able to carry large humans out of burning buildings kind of work.

In order of age, here goes the rest of the clan. Tahjay went with Nana to see the James Brown movie Get On Up, and she loved it. She also did not get to enter her own news spot because she was still slumbering when I blew in for my early morning latte/baby snuggle.

Aysia has taken up boxing…and she is mean in the ring. I am hearing there has been many an opponent who has succumbed to crouching-tiger, fetal-position hiding. We mused at how the twins are likely to rely on Aysia to chase the boys away and how they will most likely toddle after Opal like dedicated little ducklings.

Opal had a lovely lunch with her mama today, had her all to herself and she dressed up for just the occasion. She wanted you all to know that the best part of her summer has been day camp at GIAC. She just performed at the talent show and danced to circus music; and the talent show was her favorite bit of all.

Our little Esmae has great potential to be a marathon runner. She is in constant movement and simply burning up all of her calories. So, the moral of the story is swaddle snugly and feed often- every moment of every day. Our shrinking Violet is also shrinking, and quite svelte and our little Esmae is not far behind. Violet also must eat all of the time, and also is ambitious. While needing less swaddling, she has a robust set of lungs, enough for the pair of them, which can be quieted if she is fed, changed, and rocked all in the same moment.

Julia is the same as she was when they were born. A milk maid momma, doubling as a milk maid momma. She truly is all breast, a universal feeding machine. She has the process down to a science; waning moon shaped pillow, football cradling arms, and robes, also mechanical milking machines. Bam! (and) thank you for formula. I was starting to think we were going to have to call in reinforcements. Now Jukes can nurse and supplement with formula, and our tiny little treasures can begin to grow and gain weight. Julia is all Hindu Goddess Devi, and all eight of her arms are in constant motion; I am so shameless I may even ask her for a hand.

The whole family is headed to Bethany Beach on Saturday. Most of the clan will ride in their fancy new minivan, aka baby-mobile, while Leyla, Papa and Jared bring up the tail end of the caravan in the convertible. They will meet Katie, Rich, Stella and Augie on the sand. It will be a full house. Jamon will join them next Thursday in time to glance at the ocean, play a round of Pickle ball, and hold each of his babies before driving his hive home on Saturday. And then, the whole of our loves will travel home in a slightly more technologically advanced version of the wagon train. Once home, all will get settled in and make final preparations for a new school year.

So much to share, by the time I take the Village pulse something new has already come and magically gone, lending itself to a new moment and a new story. Take a pulse of your own, and find the space and time to take a plunge. Each moment bears its own alive-ness.

Big Love,

Jessica

blissful dying

To My Sweet Girl

Perhaps God is a swim in the cool waters of a spring-fed pond under a starry night full of moon, or a soft breeze that lifts clouds in filtered sunlight, or better yet a wispy ethereal float in a sea of Ceylon sky.

Perhaps God sizzles around the edges of mystery, a fiery lightning bug love, flamenco sky dancing to the rhythm of a funky guitar. I will meet you in this land of pure white light being, in this single strike of a match long ago struck.

The veil, the vast limitless universe, that which is and is not; that which holds all the secrets of time, of love, of memory. My mind rests in your sky, our souls wander freely through these universal planes. And daughter, these delicious mists will rise and I will find you star gazing on pink grass, with bubbles of sunshine floating on air; with a unicorn resting in your reflection on a quiet pond.

I will find laughter, delight and joy in witnessing you undertake your whimsical butterfly travels.

And my sweet girl, we shall sit and visit long alongside the river's flow of mystery in love and wonder, in our land of the Great Beyond. I love you and your delightful, blissful dying beyond eternity.

Loving you, Jessi

My sweet daughter, my mind will ever be open to you. In the untethered window of my mind's eye, I follow you along the wistful current of your life journey, this great migration of souls, through your backwards birthing into the eternal life waters.

Oh, Dishwasher of Street Fights

Happy Fall Leyla's Village! Grab a hot cider or a mug of chai and have a read about Leyla's world. Fall came upon us quickly and with little warning. The kiddos returned to school, followed by a happy celebration for Opal's Birthday, quickly chased by the whirlwind of wet and crisp autumn air.

Leyla has been her busy self, snapping photos of those she loves and completing full portfolios of senior photos for her friends. The photos she captured of the babies are so delicious you can almost feel their little bodies breathing in your arms. While Leyla's eye for beauty and the perfect shot are crystal clear, her eyes for open dishwasher doors are not. Sadly, this dishwasher won and Leyla and her upright gravity lost; creating a lot of bruising, and swollen feet and legs which remind me of her mother's pregnant tree feet. Leyla tried to make up a story to explain her misfortune but when she tested out, "I was in a street fight", her nurses just smiled and told her she had better come up with something more believable than that…

Jamon has graduated from fire academy!!! He has learned many valuable lessons, a few of them go something like this. Fire equipment is heavy. It is hot, on top of hot. In a smoky, fiery building you can't see a thing, not even your hands in front of your face or your feet on the ground, and breathing out of a tube is much harder than it sounds. Hyperventilating is not recommended and keep thyself low (someone please come up with a rap song). The family celebrated with grilled things and salads and some insane and delicious desserts from Nana. I might even be tempted to run into a burning building if Nana offered me a cheesecake as a reward!

For the rest of the kiddos in ascending order…the babies are amazing! They are

blissful dying

looking less and less like infants and more like babies. Esmae, not to be outdone by Leyla, got her very own doctor at Strong. Her umbilical hernia needs no surgery and can otherwise be ignored. It still makes me nervous when she cries, makes me want to hold her tiny tummy in. Violet is strong and curious and spends a lot of time just looking at everything.

Miss Opal has returned to regular counseling which has been good for her little soul. She has been busy with girlfriends and sleepovers and birthday parties and lots of play.

Aysia has also been busy with sleepovers with her best friend and is practicing with the drama club for the Little Mermaid production she is in.

Tahjay is also in a play at school and is starring as Don Pedro in Shakespeare's *Much Ado About Nothing*. It seems like play rehearsal is pretty much all of the time. It also seems that drop off and pick up of all of the kiddos at all of their extracurricular activities begins at dawn and ends way past nighttime. It's a grand thing that Jukes and Jamon upgraded to a minivan, but what they really need is a chauffeur.

In other family news, Augie is not a baby anymore. He is full on young child, all curls and questions. Stella is at Montessori and is doing wonderfully. Such a good fit for such a perfect girl. Nana can be seen most mornings rocking a baby before work, and just had skylights installed in her new home. She is staying put for the fall, though after the holidays Guatemala will welcome her for a long holiday. Papa is Papa; hanging about with tiny Alvin as company and picking bunches of flowers for Leyla. There have been date nights, and soccer games, adult sleepovers, and talk of using the old play structure as firewood. There are little girls who sleep in their own crib together at night and an entire family that enjoys a loud sound machine with waves crashing through day and night.

Wrap yourselves in colorful scarves, break out your mittens and take one last look at the brightly colored leaves before they fall from grace and meet in the great compost bin of our seasons. Gaze at the low slung cold moon and wish, for we have only moments to suspend ourselves in this vibrant animation before we leap through space and time to watch with hungry, open mouths for the first taste of a winter snow.

Big Love,

Jessica

oh, dishwasher of street fights

Fury Heart of Rainbow Land

It is time we rolled through with an update about our sweetest girl. Sadly, Leyla is currently hospitalized at Strong Memorial in Rochester. To give this event perspective, Leyla has not actually been hospitalized with illness since the first days of her diagnosis, over two years now.

Leyla is uncomfortable. Like serious cancer uncomfortable, so rude you are, Cancer, to pile on tummy aches, brain searing pain, a tree leg, kidney functions all awry and blood pressure so high, Leyla might as well be carrying two baby elephants on her back day and night. All signs point to STOP! Leyla is hanging out in her shared hospital room with Nana and Papa for company today. She will be taking deep breaths, while the doctors assess what might be causing all of this terrible-ness. What we know now is this, Leyla's brain is good; the rest of herself is not so much. One way to restore balance is to hold chemotherapy for a time, so this will be the current path forward. For while the chemotherapy has done a remarkable job in keeping Leyla's tumors stable, it is a toxic assault on the rest of her. A battery of tests will occur over the next few days to determine among other things what the causes of these symptoms seem to be; and whether there may be some other sneaky tumor bastards hanging out in Leyla's spine and if a murmur has found its way into her heart.

> There are multiple things at play here; like a complicated and high stakes match of chess, it is balance, healing, strategy and the ability to read the signs that mark the rules of this life game.

This news lights my fury-heart and makes me momentarily want to kick a rainbow, or say "fuck you" to a koala bear. When that impulse passes (and it does) it is important that we collectively take stock, assess the attitude in which we view the world. Find your gratitude, after all you are not in a hospital room sharing a bathroom with a stranger. Julia and tribe are taking

stock as well, and as one can imagine are holding their own fury-hearts at bay by shining their love in the right places. Opal is openly talking about her fears and wanted to know if Leyla would die during her visit to the hospital, as Sadie did only last year. Julia and family are inviting these questions from their little ones so that they can process this in a healthy way. They are saying to Opal, and each other, that Leyla is feeling sick right now, but she will not die. That is for a future day and a so much suckier conversation. Leyla is planning for a return home this Saturday, after the hospital has dazzled her with all that shiny, medical marvels have to offer.

Leyla and her family are holding one another close and watching as emotions float by on the waters of all time. When the time calls for it, they can fish for individual sentiments, and once caught can cherish its feel, until it is time to pass them along and move onto the next.

For now, let's gentle our minds and be grateful that information is a beautiful thing; and any information gleaned from this hospital stay will help Leyla feel better so that she can continue to live her best life. When the moon rises tonight I am going to wish on its waning form that the journey for Leyla is as long and beautiful as it is humbling.

Big Love,

Jessica & Leyla

Feel free to cast your wish in with mine, I suspect the moon can hold them all.

Photo Courtesy of Kathy Troy

Come Home Sweet Firefly

We are spinning towards the Christmas holiday with heavy hearts, and a sadness that weeps around our edges; our grief is somehow not made easier by wrapping paper and ribbons that sparkle or carefully rolled and baked confections.

In these moments our souls escape us and we must reach for one another as our souls flutter about. We collectively catch them up like fireflies, and tuck them back inside our bodies and weigh them down, with the reality of this changing situation.

Leyla, Julia, Linda and the twins trooped to Rochester today for a day of scans and appointments with a kidney specialist and Dr. Korones. Leyla's MRI today showed rapid growth of her tumor since Thanksgiving time. They chased these difficult conversations with hamburgers and clams while they pondered what's next.

Chemotherapy at a reduced dose is still an option, but needs to be carefully balanced with her compromised kidney functions and elevated blood pressure. Hospicare services have been arranged and have already begun providing supports to Leyla through a new program they have for teenagers living with cancer.

We are stranded in the stark land of hard truths, and questions were asked, and answered. Ouch, life. This feels a bit like suffocating, as though we are hurdling toward the end of a chapter that has already been carved in stone in an ancient language we cannot yet decipher.

We must skin the surface and peel away the layers to find the shiny-ness of our gratitude. We are together and therefore we are living in the bliss of our whole-ness. As Leyla is wont to say, this is "inevitable, blissful dying."

Time marches on, and Christmas Eve will be celebrated with the whole clan at Papa's with Nana ensconced in the kitchen cooking magical treats and the kiddos running here and there with the promise of Santa. Christmas Day will be a laid back affair, with Leyla and family at her house relaxing on couches and munching on deliciousness. With the New Year approaching we can look to the brightening of days and the whispers of growing things and hold close the abiding hope that we will be whole this spring.

Long ago, I created a little nest in my heart for my Leyla to reside. Each day I hold her close, and hear her voice in my head. That beautiful voice, full of optimism and kindness and wisdom reminding me that this life is precious, and sweet, and that it is a gift.

I wrap this gift in my mind's eye and stow it under my brightly lit Christmas tree. I am grateful that our wonderful Leyla, our beautiful ocean nymph, gives us these perfect life lessons, the most generous of gifts.

I asked her, "Baby, what gift do you wish for Christmas?" and she replied that she just can't get enough of the second-hand pair of leg warmers I gave her and she would love to have another pair. We would give her the moon, balanced on a silvery dolphin's head, and she wishes for leg warmers. And the gift of her seems endless, and yes, she will have more leg warmers. More than she knows what to do with.

Life bears a seemingly endless evolution of transformation, and we find ourselves on a journey full of humility, wisdom and knowing. One moment we are trapped on a soul shattering trajectory only to find ourselves, a moment later, full of hope and humility and the gift and responsibility to live our lives beautifully well, without the promise of tomorrows. So, from our souls to yours, we wish for you, more than ever: a Happy Christmas and New Year.

Big Love,

Jessica

A Daughter's Rite of Passage

With both delight and a deep well of sorrow, we wish to share that Leyla has moved into the beautiful Hospice residence. Our collective souls are feeling hijacked, and heavy, as though we have sustained a thousand splinters in our heart's center. Our girl chose carefully the things she wished to take with her on this new journey. So many vestiges of childhood stayed behind, while others reflective of the woman she has become have made their way into her new life. So, she has surrounded herself with photos, and twinkle lights, hand sewn quilts, and a turtle that shows the night sky. She took her childhood stuffed lamb, "Lamby," of course, and sky lanterns, and was

Live Life Like Leyla

delighted by aromatherapy galore. She packed all the safety socks she owned, and stuffed her drawers with the softest Soma had to offer. Papa strung the deck overlooking the pond outside her room with lights that shimmer and stuffed the bird feeder full of seed.

Leyla surprised us with her life decision to move to Hospice last week. We did not see this coming as we had planned all along that the winter of Leyla's life would be spent at her home. This decision is so very Leyla, and we are endlessly grateful that she can so clearly help us understand what her needs are and how we can best love and support her in this final transition.

Leyla has been experiencing an untenable amount of pain, so our hearts are glowing at the prospect of hospice healing her discomfort with their gift and knowledge of pain management. We have happily chatted about how her new room shines with comfort, light, and home. Leyla will be hosting sleepovers with her lovelies and soaking in the beauty of being grown and moving out on her own. Such a delightful rite of passage! We hope that Leyla will still be able to spend time at home, and at Papa's and Nana's and Katie's.

Leyla is looking forward to a quiet trip to Sanibel Island with her Nana and Papa in just two weeks. They plan on snuggling in, digging their toes in the sand, and letting the sun shine their hearts warm. We are crossing our fingers and talking to the sands of time that this will come to pass, yet another wish to rest our minds on.

Today marked a huge transition, and we are still breathing

through the newness of it all. Leyla is sure to reach out to all her loved ones as she gets settled and to happily greet visitors in the coming days. If you don't hear from Leyla or the family directly, please touch base before visiting. We want Leyla to have time to settle into her new space with her family and also allow her some time to rest while Hospice finds the best way to help her with pain management.

We are in the mists of preparing Leyla for this great migration of souls, and while our hearts are at times heavy with sadness we are basking in the beauty of the gift of Leyla and with all of the moments in time she has shined our lives bright. The love of Leyla's Village is a soul salve. It is healing, and gentle and kind. So love bright, be sweet, cry in your bodies, honor your emotions, and hold one another close. We love you and the beauty you bring to Leyla and her village. We will be in touch, and soon.

This is our life, our humanity, our primordial oneness.

Big Love,

Jessica

Twinkle Lights on Snowflake Shimmer

I am snuggled in with Leyla watching snow float quietly on the air, listening to the soft sounds of her slumber. During the brief moments of her waking she asks me, "Don't we need to write something?", and I tell her "why, of course we do…"

So, while she dances in dream land, I am writing to you of all the things she wishes to say. Leyla wants you to know she is deep-down, soul-happy and at peace with her life and her limitless future. She has made peace with the frustration of her dying body and her hiding words.

Leyla does not wish for tears, nor pity. She does not wish for drama and she does not wish to be seen as the girl who will lose her battle with cancer. In fact, she is fierce in her strength and knowledge that when she dies, her cancer will die too. Our Leyla knows her soul is destined for beautiful things and the cancer inside of her just gets death.

Leyla captures being by cherishing every single breath, and breathing love into each moment. So, in these last months, days or weeks we chat long, listen to Papa strum his guitar late into the night, drink toasty chai, delight in Nana's family dinners, and watch as Leyla tries to master the one-handed diaper change for her treasured babies. We breathe with Leyla in her beautiful space, filled with so many photos, fresh flowers, lights that twinkle, gifts of orchids, aroma therapy, delicious treats and the unlikely promise of a baby elephant. We delight in her kindness to all things, even to the squirrels who eat all of the birdseed outside her window. And she laughs brightly at these squirrels, because they are very cute and hungry too.

We are feeling so grateful for you. Particularly for the delicious meals that helped sustain Julia's hive this week, and for the loving care of the Eslets (twins) and fun water park adventure for Opal and Aysia. As the sunshine turns snowflakes into a diamond shimmer, I look at our peaceful girl deep inside her dreamland slumber and read these words hanging above her bed:

Big love, sleeping

Leyla & Jessica

> **When you realize how perfect everything is, you will tilt your head back and laugh at the sky.**
>
> —*Buddha*

Leyla's Song

Under all of this snow we have unearthed a beautiful gift for our sweet Leyla and her Village. The Blind Spots, featuring Jayhigh and Rising Sun of The Gunpoets, have been writing and singing and conjuring their magic for us these past months. It has been a delicious secret of ours that we are so excited to share with you.

So, have a listen our sweet friends to "Leyla's Song," written in the language of our love, rooting us in our memories and dancing with us beyond the veil of universal sway. We will be sharing a full update tomorrow. We have so much to be grateful for and so much to tell you all. For today, we ask you to find a quiet space to sit inside of your body and be with us as we unfold this gift together. We just know, the deliciousness of it all will drop you to you knees, and you will taste your joy.

I have no words to honor what is in my heart when I hear Leyla's song. Thank you seems almost rude it is so insufficient. I want to fill an old Volvo station wagon with all of the sunflowers and daisies that could possibly fit. I would drive this car in the spring sunshine to a wide lavender field; song playing, windows down and flower petals floating out of the windows and streaming their yellow rain on the wind. And in this thank you of my imagination, this old Volvo will come to rest in this open field. We will throw the doors wide open to the sun and pray this car who has the soundscape memory of the masters has one good speaker to play your awesome tune. We will dance and I will snuggle each of your beautiful faces and fill your arms heavy with so many flowers you will have to fall to the ground and just gaze at big sky.

In my mind's eye, you will know in this moment just how delightful and sweet you are. We love you, deep down soul shimmy joyful; and we will hold this gift of yours on a window seat in our soulhouse where it will rest in our peacefulness.

Courtesy of Dave Burbank Photography

Song for Leyla

THE BLIND SPOTS

I wish I lived by a riverside You can watch the season roll, roll, roll I wish I lived by the seaside You can watch the tide come and go I wish I lived in a high rise You can hear the neighbors' comedy show I wish I lived on the edge of a cliff Where every day you ask, "What if?"

But you'll always have one foot in this world and the other one left to dance Believe that, little girl: Your wishes are all in your hands You'll always have one foot in this world wherever it is that you land Believe that little girl She'll help you understand

I wish I lived in outer space floating without gravity I wish I lived deep in a cave where the echoes all agree with me

But you'll always have one foot in this world and the other one left to dance Believe that, little girl: Your wishes are all in your hands You'll always have one foot in this world wherever it is that you land Believe that little girl She'll help you understand

blissful dying

JAYHIGH

Back when I was caught in the "woulda, shoulda, coulda," At end of the day, I would just hide under covers. but in the morning I would take flight into the wonder-us, With the ground way under-us. And with beautiful sounds playing thunderous, and we all can dance like no one is judging us. Thunder struck never worried once about what's bugging us. So in love. Open up, so the hope can float us up. It's potent, so focus on the trust. We own the moment, but yet we fight and fuss. I need to enlighten-up And be reminded of, the truth I found when I realized I was in love, or when I saw GOD in a summer-time lightning bug. I just can't fight the rush! So I need to slow down...be unique, and peaceful, Breathe with a sigh of deep relief one day I'll just be...A memory. A gust of wind in the leaves...

RISING SUN

Dear Leyla, life's a trip but I can't make no sense of this Like every time I make a fist life slips right through my fingertips We all know that this life is beautiful but that don't make it any easier to let you go Pardon me while I open all the window so we can feel the wind blow and we'll wish on every the star in the sky Or maybe wish on your sparkling eyes What I wish for between you and I is that you'll remind us that we're alive Then we'll lift up your mom and sisters when the universe comes down to get you and it's gonna hurt but we'll be with our friends and we're gonna see you again...I wish I lived by a riverside... But you'll always have one foot in this world and the other one left to dance Believe that, little girl: Your wishes are all in your hands ...

song for leyla

Silent Skies, Long Journeys

We have so much to share, and truly so little time. Leyla has asked me to help her write a final good-bye, and promises that the next time we write, it will be her words to you. I will hold her words in my arms and place them in the center of the village as soon as she is able.

In the meantime, let me update you on the village news. This last week has illuminated the beauty of our suffering. The delight of you all, cozy warm meals, delicious treats, a date for Julia, overnights for kiddos, and snow day snuggles. Even more lovely was a spa retreat at La Tourelle for the family, our Shana has come home to nest, and there was a house crash make-over extravaganza worthy of reality television. And my friends, these are just the highlights…we are on a fast moving train, with sleeper cars, a fully stocked bar, and resident musicians. Our first stop this morning was at Opal's basketball game, where she made the first basket and her team won! All aboard.

These delights soften the stark reality of picc lines infusing drugs straight into Leyla's arteries. Expensive hydraulic tubs that should delight her with bubbles and relaxation, instead trap her inside, where she is cold and humiliated. The stuck-insideness required a rescue operation with me jumping in and nurses having to help me get her out. Words pour out of Leyla, but we can't always help her through the terrifying awareness that she is losing the ability to find her words and tie them together in meaning. Equally unbearable is Leyla's loss of knowing her own mind, and the way it connects to her body, as well as her eyesight and the ability to stand even for the briefest of moments. These ignite my fury-heart and I wonder if we will succumb to flames.

In these moments we are stripped bare. The memory of our soul-shine is a glimmer, seen from a great distance, as we stand under a silent gray sky. This hurts our hearts as though we have swallowed big sky whole, and this sky crowds the space around our hearts and we ache with sadness. The enforcer of our suffering stomps on our hopelessness with heavy boots and does not give a shit.

Our Leyla's beautiful energy-body seeks freedom in the mists. And while we ask the universe to be gentle and kind to her, we cannot escape the universal truth that the human body is imperfect in its design and sometimes just fucking rude.

In these moments of suffering we must find our tree legs, and allow our feet to root us to all of the beauty of organic matter, and the insides of Mother Earth. Our rooted tree legs secure us in the soil of this gnarly, old life journey. We turn to the old wisdoms, knowing that this is just a shimmer of our timelessness.

In moments where her body fails us, we lovingly create space around this brokenness. And we scoop her body up, and we hold each other tight, because inside of her, and each of us, lies our perfect self, full of love and light, just aching for gentle passage.

When these bodies of ours, these finite human forms, stumble and fall, reach into yourself. Gentle your arms and rock your divine, timeless selves into delicious slumber.

Big love,

Jessica

" We rest under the cold moon of this dark season and know. The surrender is coming. "

Beautiful

My friends, these are our Leyla's words. Each and every one of them. I gathered them up with the shiny truth in her eyes and placed them here for you with the trust she has given me to share with you her heart's meaning. This is pure Leyla, I am a humble typist.

Enjoy, loves.

Jessica

My Sweet Village,

My life is peaceful, I see, I feel. Happy. I have done everything I have wanted, I am full of life. Fulfilled.

This will be a horrible loss for my family, but they are amazing. When I am gone, your hearts need to be held. Hearts will be healed, my mom's heart will be healed.

I know I will see you and I think you will see me. And, even if you don't believe these things it will still be. I am going to be hanging around my Opal, all of our beautiful kids.

I want you to learn how to live, to simply live. There will be moments in life where you feel like you are going to fall. It feels like the world falls into the room. See the whole world around you, don't get stuck in this moment. I am past this place, I see the whole world. Beautiful.

I feel I have known people who are full of who they truly are. My friends. Sometimes you can just see people. I know when they are alone. People who are in love are more whole.

I have always felt, a peace of hope, a home. I want to thank everyone for giving a sense of selflessness throughout this love, this journey.

When I am gone I hope you have spirit. I truly want this village to just feel this love, be connected, because you are going to need it, too...

I am breathing, I am here, I am with you. I won't speak these words often, it is hard to find them, but they are in my heart.

Sending love, Leyla
—Blissfully Dying

Deliciously Sad Confections

It is time to greet the night, sweet village. It has been a day on top of days. The hard edge of cancer unrelenting. Today we turned a corner in a journey that has already been full of obstacles. We are trekking uphill, and we are weighed down heavy with sadness and chocolate chip cookies. We spend long hours with Leyla in a guess-my-thought game where we want to win badly, and where being a loser hurts so big.

We are buried in snow and in cold, and we are just about done with this madness. We are starved for gentle things, and we look down each street for a glimmer that says, "gentle things this way," and we walk longer, and with hope, but we do not find our promise. Instead, we find ourselves in a street fight with primordial thugs who punch us dead in our feelings. We dislike street fights so we dust our pacifist/optimist selves off in search of a soft baby duckling.

> We choose to live whenever possible in silver linings and with the comfort of one another. While heartbreaking, this journey also has an aching and slow-burning beauty.

Watching as Jamon scoops Leyla up in his arms, cradling her gently, and like a fallen baby bird settles her back into her nest. We delight in beer faeries, and doer friends, abandoned auctions and AWD vehicles that carry our bodies to meet our hearts. We have laughter and ice dancing, and Alaskan Shearling boot throwing, that actually did not break even one little thing.

We have been full with happy visits from all people Dietrich and a Katie inspired movement of flipping off those we love. We try and laugh at our own selves, in our terrible efforts and soaking wetness, in our two mamas and a baby shower debut. We dig colored lights all decked out, and metal cylinders that fly through big sky carrying our loved ones home and taste of Meadow tea promising spring.

Things are changing, as they always must, and as we knew it would. We will spare you the details, as we wish to keep elements of this journey private for Leyla. We do want you to know that we have tethered your love to us so that we don't lose it on our way up this mountain. We are repairing tires (literally) and digging in for the long haul. In many ways, we are entering a leg of

deliciously sad confections

this journey that we must trek alone. We have packed your love in our pockets. We are fortified, and guided by the gift of our instinct, the map of our ancestors alive and well in our sky mind.

Julia is tucked in with her firstborn, in borrowed socks and a sweatshirt that does not fit. High on McDonald's big breakfast and yellow curry, floating on the scents of bergamot and lemon. It is a mama/baby time, and it is perfection. Sometimes we even try to talk smack for fun, but Leyla does not allow us this small minded delight. Our girl is a soft one, gentle and sweet, but she would stick up for our feelings in a street fight any day.

Live in your soul shine. We are holding you all close and sending you so much love and light. Find a string of lights and a window; Leyla's Village is a bright twinkle in dark night.

Big Love,

Jessica

We are big-hearts-broken-open more each day and we are filling ourselves hungrily with love, laughter and peace.

blissful dying

The Plague

Dear stomach flu extraordinaire,

You have taken down the nucleus of our Village, at least 30 of my nearest and dearest people and counting. You sneak in on babies, and kiddos in the middle of play dates, you have taken down all of our mother's and our Nana and at least one Papa. I have never heard or seen so much vomit in my whole life.

      You have earned a place as the plague in our new game. Someday we will laugh at you hard, but today just go to hell. And move yourself back three places, you do not get to advance to the sunflower field.

I do not love you big at all,

Jessica

Photo courtesy of Kathy Troy

103

Rest on Gentle Wind

In the end, it was the longest and saddest and sweetest goodbye imaginable. Leyla had transcended to a timeless summer place; it was those who loved her that were trapped in the here and now, where time is still real, and every second that passed marked our grief. Leyla spoke her surrender only once, in the quiet dark of night, her words clear and true. Her eyes were unburdened by tears, her smile full of knowing, and love, and sadness and hope.

• • • • • • • • • • • • • • • • • •

The whole of our tribe joined us on the last leg of our journey together. We marked our final hours with gentleness towards one another, honoring our tears and our memories, reminding one another to just be, to cherish our time, to be curious and to sit comfortably with our sorrow and a blanket.

• • • • • • • • • • • • • • • • • •

Deep night shifted to dawn and it was here where we reached Leyla's final, gripping uphill climb. By the time the sun glistened its way across our frozen world, our girl was restful and at peace. She was snuggled deeply under covers, breathing softly in the arms of her mama who held her close.

We gathered in the Great Room and we labored. We laughed through our tears, and we breathed. In the throes of our final love push, we talked softly, cried loudly and snuggled under wool blankets. Papa played his guitar, and Nana nested in Leyla's favorite chair and sewed a quilt for August. Katie read poetry about the loveliest of birds, who then appeared; our spirit animals stayed close, marking this great transmigration of souls.

Opal carefully combed Leyla's hair, and painted her nails beautifully. Their goodbye was delicious, and sweet and soft in heart. And Julia, she held Leyla so gently, it made our souls spill out of our broken bodies and onto the floor. For in the end, as in the beginning, it is mother and daughter and their tender, wordless exchange of knowing, the organic imprint of one another so beautifully intertwined.

There were quiet snores, and whispered promises. Leyla, you don't need to be brave anymore, all of the hard work has been done, there is no more doing, and no more trying. Soon you will be free. Just rest baby, drift on the gentle wind. It is your time, sweet girl. We have wrapped up all of our love for you, now it is yours to take on your journey. Your new life awaits, and somehow, in a way we can scarcely imagine, it loves you even more than we do. Just float baby, float down the river on our sweet lullaby, let it carry you gently, softly bringing you to the sun-kissed banks of beyond.

Painting by Jorge Vascano

And our Leyla, she folded up all of the love we have and let it shine her forth. Thousands of sky lanterns descended from heaven and lifted her gently out of her tired body at dawn. We watched the bright fire of her soul shine until it was only a twinkling glimmer. When at last she was out of our sight, we learned a new truth, one our Leyla wanted us to know all along and bury deep in the soul of our bones.

In death, our wandering gypsy daughter met our ancestors on the beach in the sunshine; just a short walk in the warm white sand to her new summerhouse where her soul finds bliss still.

Blissful Dying is not a fairy tale, not a plea whispered in desperation to a frozen world. In the end there is only one final lesson, and only one thing that matters. Blissful Dying is for real; and it is full of love and grace and the deep knowing of soul. It is gentle, and kind and heartbreakingly sweet, and it was beautiful, after all.

Big Love,

Jessica

rest on gentle wind

Celebration of Life
for Leyla Dietrich
Aug 16th, 2015

Join us from Noon-4:30pm
at Taughannock Falls State Park North Shore

Celebration of Life Ceremony 1:00-1:30pm

Bring a picnic & anything you'll need
to enjoy a beautiful day.
We'll provide the *music, laughter & love!*

Find us on Facebook at Leyla's Village

Epilogue

Sweet girl, our daydreaming, wandering daughter. We wonder which corner of the universe you have chosen to reside; If you spend your timeless moments in the sunshine ocean breeze, floating in turquoise waters, or if you are among the stars that ripple around the glistening white moon, touching our world with a gravity that is oh, so, you.

We wonder if you can see the whole of the sky, and the universe, and all of the moments from the beginning to the end of all time. We wonder if you can watch the beauty of growing things as they bloom, and die, and come alive once more.

We wonder if you know that we have raised sunflowers, planted by our own hands and watered by tears steeped in our love. We wonder if you know the secrets we whisper to them in the deep dark of night.

We wonder if you have chosen a summer house by the sea, or if you rest your soul in meadows so wide they could swallow the whole earth. We wonder if you store your memories of us tucked away in a quiet place in your soul, or in a nest high in the heavens.

We wonder if you carry the love we feel for you in your faraway life; or if you are even far away at all. Perhaps you are the love which burns brightly in our souls and steals our breath away, and restores it once more.

We wonder if you have chosen to spend your eternity in the beauty-filled, peaceful stillness of the great beyond; or if your gypsy feet have led you back to the eternal womb where

you may choose another family to bless with your wistful, dreamy soul.

We wonder if universal love, the pure essence of light and being is even a fraction of how much we love you, how much we miss you, how much you inhabit our today and all of our tomorrows. We wonder if you have come to understand that we traveled the great expanse of worlds and lifetimes to find you, and one another.

We wonder if you see us now, where forest clearing meets water's edge, and music rises off green grass to meet the sun that rests in a clear blue sky. We wonder if you can see the shimmy that rises happily from our toes and shivers out of our fingers as we sway in the soft breeze.

We wonder if you can see how our love seeps out of our bodies and into the air full of summer. How our love plays among blades of soft green grass, and handmade quilts, and climbs trees dressed in sunflowers, and rises in bubbles of foam on top of chilly beer.

We wonder if you can see that our love peeks out of our bodies and hides cleverly, tucking itself in the deep ridges of bark and high in branches where it disguises itself as leaves. Our love floats on the water and soaks a giant fallen tree which has become a playground for our slippery fish children.

We wonder if you can see that our love climbs out of our hearts, leaving the door wide open. It reaches up on our breath and rests heavily behind our eyes, until it gathers around itself and falls.

blissful dying

Our love trickles off our feet and seeps inside the rich dark soil into the place where the earth is born.

We wonder if you know that we have searched for you in spring fed ponds and on the underside of flower blossoms, and that we have talked with beautiful things for news of you. We wonder if you know that we have dug deeply into the earth to consider the origin of where you have grown. We have let this question settle deeply into our minds, and find that in the answer that we have come to learn something new about this journey of being alive.

We have come to know that we did not lose or misplace you; rather that we set you free, only to find that you are both here and there and that these things are both simultaneous and utterly simple. We are inside of our own infinity, where we find ourselves whole, having dreamed and lived the biggest, most heartbreaking love there ever has been in any universe. Ever.

Big love,

Jessica

epilogue

Live Life Like Leyla

live life like leyla

Consultation & Support

The trajectory of Blissful Dying was set in motion around an otherwise unremarkable, albeit wobbly, table in the remarkable Ithaca Bakery over steaming dark roast coffee with friends and friends of friends on a sunny day, surrounded by hippies and hipsters and delicious food with snappy, happy names.

In this real-life story there was a single moment that our dream came to life, walking clear as day into our reality. It came to us in the form of a statement from our new friends:

"This is a love story." I fell in love in that moment with this new truth just as hopelessly as I fell in love with each of you.

Julia Dietrich, Audrey Cooper, Sara Hess, Jeff Furman, and Norma Gutierrez, you bring form to the formless, create sanity in the vastness, and bring your brilliant minds into social-action, making this world a brighter, more tender, and exquisite place. Thank you for your love, guidance and endless stream of clarity and support in making Leyla's last wish a boundless reality. As Leyla would say, "I love you, and you, and you."

Achnowledgements

Honoring Leyla's Village and the many donors who made this book possible:

T-Burg Takes on Pediatric Cancer

A local group of dedicated peope doing our part
to raise funds for pediatric cancer research and to support
those families suffering though pediatric cancer.

Ben & Jerry's Fund

The mission of the Ben & Jerry's Foundation is to engage Ben & Jerry's
employees in philanthropy and social change work; to give back to our
Vermont communities; and to support grassroots activism and
community organizing for social and environmental justice around the country.

Reach Out to Leyla's Village!

blissfuldying.leylasvillage@gmail.com

live life like leyla

Made in the USA
Charleston, SC
09 September 2016